VIVIAN TENORIO

PLAYING PRETEND
LAW OF ATTRACTION PLANNER
I've decided to live the life I've always wanted

life scripted and lived by: *Sarah Nevine*

VIVIAN TENORIO

PLAYING PRETEND
LAW OF ATTRACTION PLANNER
I've decided to live the life I've always wanted

BY VIVIAN TENORIO

JAV PUBLISHING

Printed in the United Stated of America

www.viviantenorio.com

ISBN-10: **1542798582**
ISBN-13: **978-1542798587**

Ever dream about creating a completely different life? Do you believe in the Law of Attraction? If so, you may as well know that the #1 rule of the Law of Attraction is to "feel as if" to live as if that of which you desire is already here present.

This Play Pretend Journal is designed for just that. It's the tool you need to journal with, visualize and document the life you want to manifest as if it was already here.

Inside you will find a guided journal with the 3 steps you can follow daily to help you manifest your true life. Use the journal daily, journal as if the things that you want just happened today. Think of this journal as your Play Pretend journal or even a parallel life journal. You'll journal not your real life and what really happened today, but the pretend life.

Think of it like this... re-write your day how you wished it would have played out. This is your script and the life you will live. It will start in your dreams then move into this journal and then into existence.

Share in vivid detail. Tell the journal about the weather, what you ate for lunch, who you spoke with, what you're working on. It will help you feel it, see it, experience it and day dream your life into existence.

"Everything in this journal shall come to be" *with love, Vivian*

LAW OF ATTRACTION – STEPS FOR USING THIS JOURNAL

Step 1: Play Pretend

Journal your entire day in great detail. Tell me how good your green juice was. Tell me what happened when you called your best friend.

-Jan 30, 2017 Today was one of the best days yet. I stopped by the cycle studio and got my workout on! lol I'm starting to really see results from my workouts, and it feels good. I love my body when it looks this way. I picked up a few things at Target. They have a new organic cereal that I cant wait to try in the morning. I know that feeding my body the best food is key to an amazing life. Jennifer called and told me she was leaving Mike. What! What...tell you more tomorrow after we have dinner. Love Vivian ps. Thank you for my life. xoxo

STEP 2: SPEND WITHOUT WORRY

Everyday journal what you purchased with a pretend $1,000. You can't save any money for the next day, you must use it in the day it is given. Every day increase the amount by multiplying the amount from the day before by 2.

Example: Day 1 spend $1,000
Day 2 spend $2,000
Day 3 spend $4,000

This will help with your imagination. If you had the real money what would you do with it.

Step 3: Receive

"Everything that is in this journal, shall come to be." { period }

Tell me if you see evidence of your pretend life in your real life. Be grateful and notice even the smallest evidence of the law of attraction. The more you are grateful and paying attention, the faster your desires will manifests.

Tools & Tips

Write each day in first person

Writing in first person means **writing** from the author's point of view or perspective. This point of view is used for autobiographical **writing** as well as narrative. The **first person** is an alternative to second **person**, which uses "you," as in the sentence "You are the smartest **person** in the room."

Play Pretend, journal what you eat, who you spoke with, what you shopped for. Make-believe, imagination, role-playing

Play the picture in your mind - focus on the life you want.

Don't be shy, this is your journal, no one else should read it.

Feel the joy - feel the happiness :o)

Gratitude will bring more into our lives immediately.

Remember this is your dream life, don't hold back. You have endless possibilities.

Learn to become still .. and take your attention away from what you don't want, and place your attention on what you wish to experience.

When you have an inspired thought, you must trust it and act on it.

Create a Vision Board .. pictures of what you want to attract .. every day look at it and get into the feeling state of already having acquired these wants.

STEP 1: PLAY PRETEND

Journal your entire day in great detail. Tell me how good your green juice was. Tell me what happened when you called your best friend.

This morning was so good - I really enjoyed getting dressed and ready. I pulled on my size 10 skinny jeans with such ease - I enjoyed walking around in my jeans and bra and noticing my toned waist and stomach in the mirror as well as my perky boobs and slim, toned arms and shoulders.

I enjoyed the feeling and look of my body and my beautiful face.

I enjoy how young and beautiful I am.

It's a day off and I have a lunch date with my sexy man.

I'm meeting him at a really nice restaurant - he loves to buy me nice things, It's nice popping to meet him and having a nice day off to shop, and get a massage and leisurly walk around.

I love that we plan to move in together soon, but for now I'm really enjoying the excitment of meeting up with him and dressing up my toned, slim body in sexy, stylish clothes and cute heels. - We love each other so much. I feel so happy and so safe and secure - In love, financers, friendships and in my own skin. I love my beautiful face and body - my health, my lifestyle - my career, my man, my friends - my family.

I'm so blessed.

Real Date: 28th June 17.

STEP 2: SPEND WITHOUT WORRY ☀

Everyday journal what you purchased with a pretend $1,000. You can't save any money for the next day, you must use it in the day it is given. Everyday increase the amount by multiplying the amount from the day before by 2.

I put it straight into my account to pay my rent on friday - and to pay damo back the £250.

I also put £350 aside for my treatment on thesday and £60. for wednesday - it feels so great to be secure and to know I now have more than enough money to cover my expenses.

Total Purchased Today: $ __1000.__

Step 3: Receive ☀

"Everything that is in this journal, shall come to be."

Tell me if you see evidence of your pretend life in your real life. Be grateful and notice even the smallest evidence of the law of attraction. The more you are grateful and paying attention, the faster your desires will manifests.

"I have evidence of my abundance in my real life."

Real Date: _____

I do feel beaueful today - I'm getting treatmens to be even more outragly beauful. Money is coming in. - I do get leisure time between work - I do have a nice lifestyle.

STEP 1: PLAY PRETEND

Journal your entire day in great detail. Tell me how good your green juice was. Tell me what happened when you called your best friend.

_____

_____

_____

_____

_____

_____

_____

_____

_____

_____

_____

_____

_____

_____

_____

_____

_____

_____

_____

_____

_____

_____

_____

_____

_____

_____

_____

_____

Real Date: _____

STEP 2: SPEND WITHOUT WORRY ☀

Everyday journal what you purchased with a pretend $1,000. You can't save any money for the next day, you must use it in the day it is given. Everyday increase the amount by multiplying the amount from the day before by 2.

_____

_____

_____

_____

_____

_____

_____

_____

Total Purchased Today: $_____

Step 3: Receive ☀

"Everything that is in this journal, shall come to be."

Tell me if you see evidence of your pretend life in your real life. Be grateful and notice even the smallest evidence of the law of attraction. The more you are grateful and paying attention, the faster your desires will manifests.

"I have evidence of my abundance in my real life."

Real Date: _____

_____

_____

_____

_____

_____

_____

_____

_____

_____

_____

_____

STEP 1: PLAY PRETEND

Journal your entire day in great detail. Tell me how good your green juice was. Tell me what happened when you called your best friend.

_____
_____
_____
_____
_____
_____
_____
_____
_____
_____
_____
_____
_____
_____
_____
_____
_____
_____
_____
_____
_____
_____
_____
_____
_____
_____
_____
_____
_____
_____
_____

Real Date: _____

STEP 2: SPEND WITHOUT WORRY ☼

Everyday journal what you purchased with a pretend $1,000. You can't save any money for the next day, you must use it in the day it is given. Everyday increase the amount by multiplying the amount from the day before by 2.

_____
_____
_____
_____
_____
_____
_____
_____
_____

Total Purchased Today: $_____

Step 3: Receive ☺

"Everything that is in this journal, shall come to be."

Tell me if you see evidence of your pretend life in your real life. Be grateful and notice even the smallest evidence of the law of attraction. The more you are grateful and paying attention, the faster your desires will manifests.

"I have evidence of my abundance in my real life."

Real Date: _____

_____
_____
_____
_____
_____
_____
_____
_____
_____
_____
_____
_____

STEP 1: PLAY PRETEND

Journal your entire day in great detail. Tell me how good your green juice was. Tell me what happened when you called your best friend.

_____
_____
_____
_____
_____
_____
_____
_____
_____
_____
_____
_____
_____
_____
_____
_____
_____
_____
_____
_____
_____
_____
_____
_____
_____
_____
_____
_____
_____

Real Date: _____

STEP 2: SPEND WITHOUT WORRY ☀

Everyday journal what you purchased with a pretend $1,000. You can't save any money for the next day, you must use it in the day it is given. Everyday increase the amount by multiplying the amount from the day before by 2.

_____
_____
_____
_____
_____
_____
_____
_____

Total Purchased Today: $_____

Step 3: Receive ☀

"Everything that is in this journal, shall come to be."
Tell me if you see evidence of your pretend life in your real life. Be grateful and notice even the smallest evidence of the law of attraction. The more you are grateful and paying attention, the faster your desires will manifests.

"I have evidence of my abundance in my real life."

Real Date: _____

_____
_____
_____
_____
_____
_____
_____
_____
_____
_____
_____

STEP 1: PLAY PRETEND

Journal your entire day in great detail. Tell me how good your green juice was. Tell me what happened when you called your best friend.

Real Date: _____

STEP 2: SPEND WITHOUT WORRY ☀

Everyday journal what you purchased with a pretend $1,000. You can't save any money for the next day, you must use it in the day it is given. Everyday increase the amount by multiplying the amount from the day before by 2.

_____

_____

_____

_____

_____

_____

_____

_____

_____

Total Purchased Today: $_____

Step 3: Receive ☀

"Everything that is in this journal, shall come to be."

Tell me if you see evidence of your pretend life in your real life. Be grateful and notice even the smallest evidence of the law of attraction. The more you are grateful and paying attention, the faster your desires will manifests.

"I have evidence of my abundance in my real life."

Real Date: _____

_____

_____

_____

_____

_____

_____

_____

_____

_____

_____

_____

STEP 1: PLAY PRETEND

Journal your entire day in great detail. Tell me how good your green juice was. Tell me what happened when you called your best friend.

_____

_____

_____

_____

_____

_____

_____

_____

_____

_____

_____

_____

_____

_____

_____

_____

_____

_____

_____

_____

_____

_____

_____

_____

_____

_____

_____

_____

_____

Real Date: _____

STEP 2: SPEND WITHOUT WORRY ☼

Everyday journal what you purchased with a pretend $1,000. You can't save any money for the next day, you must use it in the day it is given. Everyday increase the amount by multiplying the amount from the day before by 2.

_____

_____

_____

_____

_____

_____

_____

_____

Total Purchased Today: $_____

Step 3: Receive ☼

"Everything that is in this journal, shall come to be."

Tell me if you see evidence of your pretend life in your real life. Be grateful and notice even the smallest evidence of the law of attraction. The more you are grateful and paying attention, the faster your desires will manifests.

"I have evidence of my abundance in my real life."

Real Date: _____

_____

_____

_____

_____

_____

_____

_____

_____

_____

_____

_____

STEP 1: PLAY PRETEND

Journal your entire day in great detail. Tell me how good your green juice was. Tell me what happened when you called your best friend.

_____
_____
_____
_____
_____
_____
_____
_____
_____
_____
_____
_____
_____
_____
_____
_____
_____
_____
_____
_____
_____
_____
_____
_____
_____
_____
_____
_____
_____
_____
_____

Real Date: _____

STEP 2: SPEND WITHOUT WORRY ☼

Everyday journal what you purchased with a pretend $1,000. You can't save any money for the next day, you must use it in the day it is given. Everyday increase the amount by multiplying the amount from the day before by 2.

_____

_____

_____

_____

_____

_____

_____

_____

Total Purchased Today: $_____

Step 3: Receive ☼

"Everything that is in this journal, shall come to be."

Tell me if you see evidence of your pretend life in your real life. Be grateful and notice even the smallest evidence of the law of attraction. The more you are grateful and paying attention, the faster your desires will manifests.

"I have evidence of my abundance in my real life."

Real Date: _____

_____

_____

_____

_____

_____

_____

_____

_____

_____

_____

_____

STEP 1: PLAY PRETEND 🐝

Journal your entire day in great detail. Tell me how good your green juice was. Tell me what happened when you called your best friend.

_____

_____

_____

_____

_____

_____

_____

_____

_____

_____

_____

_____

_____

_____

_____

_____

_____

_____

_____

_____

_____

_____

_____

_____

_____

_____

_____

_____

_____

_____

_____

_____

_____

Real Date: _____

STEP 2: SPEND WITHOUT WORRY ☀

Everyday journal what you purchased with a pretend $1,000. You can't save any money for the next day, you must use it in the day it is given. Everyday increase the amount by multiplying the amount from the day before by 2.

_____
_____
_____
_____
_____
_____
_____
_____

Total Purchased Today: $_____

Step 3: Receive ☀

"Everything that is in this journal, shall come to be."

Tell me if you see evidence of your pretend life in your real life. Be grateful and notice even the smallest evidence of the law of attraction. The more you are grateful and paying attention, the faster your desires will manifests.

"I have evidence of my abundance in my real life."

Real Date: _____

_____
_____
_____
_____
_____
_____
_____
_____
_____
_____
_____
_____

STEP 1: PLAY PRETEND

Journal your entire day in great detail. Tell me how good your green juice was. Tell me what happened when you called your best friend.

_____
_____
_____
_____
_____
_____
_____
_____
_____
_____
_____
_____
_____
_____
_____
_____
_____
_____
_____
_____
_____
_____
_____
_____
_____
_____
_____
_____

Real Date: _____

STEP 2: SPEND WITHOUT WORRY ☼

Everyday journal what you purchased with a pretend $1,000. You can't save any money for the next day, you must use it in the day it is given. Everyday increase the amount by multiplying the amount from the day before by 2.

_____
_____
_____
_____
_____
_____
_____
_____

Total Purchased Today: $_____

Step 3: Receive ☼

"Everything that is in this journal, shall come to be."

Tell me if you see evidence of your pretend life in your real life. Be grateful and notice even the smallest evidence of the law of attraction. The more you are grateful and paying attention, the faster your desires will manifests.

"I have evidence of my abundance in my real life."

Real Date: _____

_____
_____
_____
_____
_____
_____
_____
_____
_____
_____
_____

STEP 1: PLAY PRETEND

Journal your entire day in great detail. Tell me how good your green juice was. Tell me what happened when you called your best friend.

_____

_____

_____

_____

_____

_____

_____

_____

_____

_____

_____

_____

_____

_____

_____

_____

_____

_____

_____

_____

_____

_____

_____

_____

_____

_____

_____

Real Date: _____

STEP 2: SPEND WITHOUT WORRY ☀

Everyday journal what you purchased with a pretend $1,000. You can't save any money for the next day, you must use it in the day it is given. Everyday increase the amount by multiplying the amount from the day before by 2.

_____
_____
_____
_____
_____
_____
_____
_____
_____

Total Purchased Today: $_____

Step 3: Receive ☀

"Everything that is in this journal, shall come to be."
Tell me if you see evidence of your pretend life in your real life. Be grateful and notice even the smallest evidence of the law of attraction. The more you are grateful and paying attention, the faster your desires will manifests.

"I have evidence of my abundance in my real life."

Real Date: _____

_____
_____
_____
_____
_____
_____
_____
_____
_____
_____
_____

STEP 1: PLAY PRETEND

Journal your entire day in great detail. Tell me how good your green juice was. Tell me what happened when you called your best friend.

_____
_____
_____
_____
_____
_____
_____
_____
_____
_____
_____
_____
_____
_____
_____
_____
_____
_____
_____
_____
_____
_____
_____
_____
_____
_____
_____

Real Date: _____

STEP 2: SPEND WITHOUT WORRY ☼

Everyday journal what you purchased with a pretend $1,000. You can't save any money for the next day, you must use it in the day it is given. Everyday increase the amount by multiplying the amount from the day before by 2.

_____

_____

_____

_____

_____

_____

_____

_____

_____

Total Purchased Today: $_____

Step 3: Receive ☺

"Everything that is in this journal, shall come to be."

Tell me if you see evidence of your pretend life in your real life. Be grateful and notice even the smallest evidence of the law of attraction. The more you are grateful and paying attention, the faster your desires will manifests.

"I have evidence of my abundance in my real life."

Real Date: _____

_____

_____

_____

_____

_____

_____

_____

_____

_____

_____

_____

STEP 1: PLAY PRETEND

Journal your entire day in great detail. Tell me how good your green juice was. Tell me what happened when you called your best friend.

_____
_____
_____
_____
_____
_____
_____
_____
_____
_____
_____
_____
_____
_____
_____
_____
_____
_____
_____
_____
_____
_____
_____
_____
_____
_____
_____
_____
_____

Real Date: _____

STEP 2: SPEND WITHOUT WORRY ☀

Everyday journal what you purchased with a pretend $1,000. You can't save any money for the next day, you must use it in the day it is given. Everyday increase the amount by multiplying the amount from the day before by 2.

_____

_____

_____

_____

_____

_____

_____

_____

_____

Total Purchased Today: $_____

Step 3: Receive ☀

"Everything that is in this journal, shall come to be."

Tell me if you see evidence of your pretend life in your real life. Be grateful and notice even the smallest evidence of the law of attraction. The more you are grateful and paying attention, the faster your desires will manifests.

"I have evidence of my abundance in my real life."

Real Date: _____

_____

_____

_____

_____

_____

_____

_____

_____

_____

_____

_____

_____

STEP 1: PLAY PRETEND

Journal your entire day in great detail. Tell me how good your green juice was. Tell me what happened when you called your best friend.

_____
_____
_____
_____
_____
_____
_____
_____
_____
_____
_____
_____
_____
_____
_____
_____
_____
_____
_____
_____
_____
_____
_____
_____
_____
_____
_____
_____
_____
_____
_____
_____

Real Date: _____

STEP 2: SPEND WITHOUT WORRY ☼

Everyday journal what you purchased with a pretend $1,000. You can't save any money for the next day, you must use it in the day it is given. Everyday increase the amount by multiplying the amount from the day before by 2.

_____

_____

_____

_____

_____

_____

_____

_____

_____

Total Purchased Today: $_____

Step 3: Receive 🔆

"Everything that is in this journal, shall come to be."

Tell me if you see evidence of your pretend life in your real life. Be grateful and notice even the smallest evidence of the law of attraction. The more you are grateful and paying attention, the faster your desires will manifests.

"I have evidence of my abundance in my real life."

Real Date: _____

_____

_____

_____

_____

_____

_____

_____

_____

_____

_____

_____

STEP 1: PLAY PRETEND 🐝

Journal your entire day in great detail. Tell me how good your green juice was. Tell me what happened when you called your best friend.

Real Date: _____

STEP 2: SPEND WITHOUT WORRY ☼

Everyday journal what you purchased with a pretend $1,000. You can't save any money for the next day, you must use it in the day it is given. Everyday increase the amount by multiplying the amount from the day before by 2.

_____

_____

_____

_____

_____

_____

_____

_____

Total Purchased Today: $_____

Step 3: Receive ☼

"Everything that is in this journal, shall come to be."
Tell me if you see evidence of your pretend life in your real life. Be grateful and notice even the smallest evidence of the law of attraction. The more you are grateful and paying attention, the faster your desires will manifests.

"I have evidence of my abundance in my real life."

Real Date: _____

_____

_____

_____

_____

_____

_____

_____

_____

_____

_____

_____

STEP 1: PLAY PRETEND

Journal your entire day in great detail. Tell me how good your green juice was. Tell me what happened when you called your best friend.

_____
_____
_____
_____
_____
_____
_____
_____
_____
_____
_____
_____
_____
_____
_____
_____
_____
_____
_____
_____
_____
_____
_____
_____
_____
_____
_____
_____
_____
_____
_____
_____
_____

Real Date: _____

STEP 2: SPEND WITHOUT WORRY ☀

Everyday journal what you purchased with a pretend $1,000. You can't save any money for the next day, you must use it in the day it is given. Everyday increase the amount by multiplying the amount from the day before by 2.

_____

_____

_____

_____

_____

_____

_____

_____

Total Purchased Today: $_____

Step 3: Receive ☺

"Everything that is in this journal, shall come to be."

Tell me if you see evidence of your pretend life in your real life. Be grateful and notice even the smallest evidence of the law of attraction. The more you are grateful and paying attention, the faster your desires will manifests.

"I have evidence of my abundance in my real life."

Real Date: _____

_____

_____

_____

_____

_____

_____

_____

_____

_____

_____

_____

STEP 1: PLAY PRETEND

Journal your entire day in great detail. Tell me how good your green juice was. Tell me what happened when you called your best friend.

_____

_____

_____

_____

_____

_____

_____

_____

_____

_____

_____

_____

_____

_____

_____

_____

_____

_____

_____

_____

_____

_____

_____

_____

_____

_____

_____

_____

_____

_____

Real Date: _____

STEP 2: SPEND WITHOUT WORRY ☀

Everyday journal what you purchased with a pretend $1,000. You can't save any money for the next day, you must use it in the day it is given. Everyday increase the amount by multiplying the amount from the day before by 2.

_____
_____
_____
_____
_____
_____
_____
_____
_____

Total Purchased Today: $_____

Step 3: Receive ☀

"Everything that is in this journal, shall come to be."

Tell me if you see evidence of your pretend life in your real life. Be grateful and notice even the smallest evidence of the law of attraction. The more you are grateful and paying attention, the faster your desires will manifests.

"I have evidence of my abundance in my real life."

Real Date: _____

_____
_____
_____
_____
_____
_____
_____
_____
_____
_____
_____
_____

STEP 1: PLAY PRETEND

Journal your entire day in great detail. Tell me how good your green juice was. Tell me what happened when you called your best friend.

_____
_____
_____
_____
_____
_____
_____
_____
_____
_____
_____
_____
_____
_____
_____
_____
_____
_____
_____
_____
_____
_____
_____
_____
_____
_____
_____
_____
_____
_____

Real Date: _____

STEP 2: SPEND WITHOUT WORRY ☼

Everyday journal what you purchased with a pretend $1,000. You can't save any money for the next day, you must use it in the day it is given. Everyday increase the amount by multiplying the amount from the day before by 2.

_____
_____
_____
_____
_____
_____
_____
_____

_____

Total Purchased Today: $_____

Step 3: Receive ☼

"Everything that is in this journal, shall come to be."
Tell me if you see evidence of your pretend life in your real life. Be grateful and notice even the smallest evidence of the law of attraction. The more you are grateful and paying attention, the faster your desires will manifests.

"I have evidence of my abundance in my real life."

Real Date: _____

_____
_____
_____
_____
_____
_____
_____
_____
_____
_____
_____
_____

STEP 1: PLAY PRETEND

Journal your entire day in great detail. Tell me how good your green juice was. Tell me what happened when you called your best friend.

_____
_____
_____
_____
_____
_____
_____
_____
_____
_____
_____
_____
_____
_____
_____
_____
_____
_____
_____
_____
_____
_____
_____
_____
_____
_____
_____
_____
_____
_____
_____
_____

Real Date: _____

STEP 2: SPEND WITHOUT WORRY ☀

Everyday journal what you purchased with a pretend $1,000. You can't save any money for the next day, you must use it in the day it is given. Everyday increase the amount by multiplying the amount from the day before by 2.

_____

_____

_____

_____

_____

_____

_____

_____

Total Purchased Today: $_____

Step 3: Receive ☺

"Everything that is in this journal, shall come to be."

Tell me if you see evidence of your pretend life in your real life. Be grateful and notice even the smallest evidence of the law of attraction. The more you are grateful and paying attention, the faster your desires will manifests.

"I have evidence of my abundance in my real life."

Real Date: _____

_____

_____

_____

_____

_____

_____

_____

_____

_____

_____

_____

STEP 1: PLAY PRETEND

Journal your entire day in great detail. Tell me how good your green juice was. Tell me what happened when you called your best friend.

_____

_____

_____

_____

_____

_____

_____

_____

_____

_____

_____

_____

_____

_____

_____

_____

_____

_____

_____

_____

_____

_____

_____

_____

_____

_____

_____

_____

_____

_____

Real Date: _____

STEP 2: SPEND WITHOUT WORRY ☀

Everyday journal what you purchased with a pretend $1,000. You can't save any money for the next day, you must use it in the day it is given. Everyday increase the amount by multiplying the amount from the day before by 2.

_____

_____

_____

_____

_____

_____

_____

_____

Total Purchased Today: $_____

Step 3: Receive ☺

"Everything that is in this journal, shall come to be."

Tell me if you see evidence of your pretend life in your real life. Be grateful and notice even the smallest evidence of the law of attraction. The more you are grateful and paying attention, the faster your desires will manifests.

"I have evidence of my abundance in my real life."

Real Date: _____

_____

_____

_____

_____

_____

_____

_____

_____

_____

_____

_____

STEP 1: PLAY PRETEND

Journal your entire day in great detail. Tell me how good your green juice was. Tell me what happened when you called your best friend.

_____
_____
_____
_____
_____
_____
_____
_____
_____
_____
_____
_____
_____
_____
_____
_____
_____
_____
_____
_____
_____
_____
_____
_____
_____
_____
_____
_____

Real Date: _____

STEP 2: SPEND WITHOUT WORRY ☼

Everyday journal what you purchased with a pretend $1,000. You can't save any money for the next day, you must use it in the day it is given. Everyday increase the amount by multiplying the amount from the day before by 2.

_____

_____

_____

_____

_____

_____

_____

_____

_____

Total Purchased Today: $_____

Step 3: Receive ☺

"Everything that is in this journal, shall come to be."

Tell me if you see evidence of your pretend life in your real life. Be grateful and notice even the smallest evidence of the law of attraction. The more you are grateful and paying attention, the faster your desires will manifests.

"I have evidence of my abundance in my real life."

Real Date: _____

_____

_____

_____

_____

_____

_____

_____

_____

_____

_____

_____

STEP 1: PLAY PRETEND

Journal your entire day in great detail. Tell me how good your green juice was. Tell me what happened when you called your best friend.

_____

_____

_____

_____

_____

_____

_____

_____

_____

_____

_____

_____

_____

_____

_____

_____

_____

_____

_____

_____

_____

_____

_____

_____

_____

_____

_____

_____

Real Date: _____

STEP 2: SPEND WITHOUT WORRY ☼

Everyday journal what you purchased with a pretend $1,000. You can't save any money for the next day, you must use it in the day it is given. Everyday increase the amount by multiplying the amount from the day before by 2.

_____
_____
_____
_____
_____
_____
_____
_____
_____

Total Purchased Today: $_____

Step 3: Receive ☺

"Everything that is in this journal, shall come to be."

Tell me if you see evidence of your pretend life in your real life. Be grateful and notice even the smallest evidence of the law of attraction. The more you are grateful and paying attention, the faster your desires will manifests.

"I have evidence of my abundance in my real life."

Real Date: _____

_____
_____
_____
_____
_____
_____
_____
_____
_____
_____
_____
_____

STEP 1: PLAY PRETEND

Journal your entire day in great detail. Tell me how good your green juice was. Tell me what happened when you called your best friend.

_____

_____

_____

_____

_____

_____

_____

_____

_____

_____

_____

_____

_____

_____

_____

_____

_____

_____

_____

_____

_____

_____

_____

_____

_____

_____

_____

Real Date: _____

STEP 2: SPEND WITHOUT WORRY ☼

Everyday journal what you purchased with a pretend $1,000. You can't save any money for the next day, you must use it in the day it is given. Everyday increase the amount by multiplying the amount from the day before by 2.

_____

_____

_____

_____

_____

_____

_____

_____

_____

Total Purchased Today: $_____

Step 3: Receive ☼

"Everything that is in this journal, shall come to be."

Tell me if you see evidence of your pretend life in your real life. Be grateful and notice even the smallest evidence of the law of attraction. The more you are grateful and paying attention, the faster your desires will manifests.

"I have evidence of my abundance in my real life."

Real Date: _____

_____

_____

_____

_____

_____

_____

_____

_____

_____

_____

_____

STEP 1: PLAY PRETEND

Journal your entire day in great detail. Tell me how good your green juice was. Tell me what happened when you called your best friend.

_____

_____

_____

_____

_____

_____

_____

_____

_____

_____

_____

_____

_____

_____

_____

_____

_____

_____

_____

_____

_____

_____

_____

_____

_____

_____

_____

_____

_____

Real Date: _____

STEP 2: SPEND WITHOUT WORRY ☀

Everyday journal what you purchased with a pretend $1,000. You can't save any money for the next day, you must use it in the day it is given. Everyday increase the amount by multiplying the amount from the day before by 2.

_____
_____
_____
_____
_____
_____
_____
_____

Total Purchased Today: $_____

Step 3: Receive ☀

"Everything that is in this journal, shall come to be."

Tell me if you see evidence of your pretend life in your real life. Be grateful and notice even the smallest evidence of the law of attraction. The more you are grateful and paying attention, the faster your desires will manifests.

"I have evidence of my abundance in my real life."

Real Date: _____

_____
_____
_____
_____
_____
_____
_____
_____
_____
_____
_____

STEP 1: PLAY PRETEND

Journal your entire day in great detail. Tell me how good your green juice was. Tell me what happened when you called your best friend.

_____
_____
_____
_____
_____
_____
_____
_____
_____
_____
_____
_____
_____
_____
_____
_____
_____
_____
_____
_____
_____
_____
_____
_____
_____
_____
_____
_____
_____
_____
_____

Real Date: _____

STEP 2: SPEND WITHOUT WORRY ☼

Everyday journal what you purchased with a pretend $1,000. You can't save any money for the next day, you must use it in the day it is given. Everyday increase the amount by multiplying the amount from the day before by 2.

_____

_____

_____

_____

_____

_____

_____

_____

Total Purchased Today: $_____

Step 3: Receive ☼

"Everything that is in this journal, shall come to be."

Tell me if you see evidence of your pretend life in your real life. Be grateful and notice even the smallest evidence of the law of attraction. The more you are grateful and paying attention, the faster your desires will manifests.

"I have evidence of my abundance in my real life."

Real Date: _____

_____

_____

_____

_____

_____

_____

_____

_____

_____

_____

_____

STEP 1: PLAY PRETEND

Journal your entire day in great detail. Tell me how good your green juice was. Tell me what happened when you called your best friend.

_____
_____
_____
_____
_____
_____
_____
_____
_____
_____
_____
_____
_____
_____
_____
_____
_____
_____
_____
_____
_____
_____
_____
_____
_____
_____
_____
_____

Real Date: _____

STEP 2: SPEND WITHOUT WORRY ☀

Everyday journal what you purchased with a pretend $1,000. You can't save any money for the next day, you must use it in the day it is given. Everyday increase the amount by multiplying the amount from the day before by 2.

_____

_____

_____

_____

_____

_____

_____

_____

_____

Total Purchased Today: $_____

Step 3: Receive ☀

"Everything that is in this journal, shall come to be."

Tell me if you see evidence of your pretend life in your real life. Be grateful and notice even the smallest evidence of the law of attraction. The more you are grateful and paying attention, the faster your desires will manifests.

"I have evidence of my abundance in my real life."

Real Date: _____

_____

_____

_____

_____

_____

_____

_____

_____

_____

_____

_____

STEP 1: PLAY PRETEND

Journal your entire day in great detail. Tell me how good your green juice was. Tell me what happened when you called your best friend.

_____
_____
_____
_____
_____
_____
_____
_____
_____
_____
_____
_____
_____
_____
_____
_____
_____
_____
_____
_____
_____
_____
_____
_____
_____
_____
_____
_____
_____

Real Date: _____

STEP 2: SPEND WITHOUT WORRY ☀

Everyday journal what you purchased with a pretend $1,000. You can't save any money for the next day, you must use it in the day it is given. Everyday increase the amount by multiplying the amount from the day before by 2.

_____

_____

_____

_____

_____

_____

_____

_____

_____

Total Purchased Today: $_____

Step 3: Receive ☺

"Everything that is in this journal, shall come to be."

Tell me if you see evidence of your pretend life in your real life. Be grateful and notice even the smallest evidence of the law of attraction. The more you are grateful and paying attention, the faster your desires will manifests.

"I have evidence of my abundance in my real life."

Real Date: _____

_____

_____

_____

_____

_____

_____

_____

_____

_____

_____

_____

STEP 1: PLAY PRETEND

Journal your entire day in great detail. Tell me how good your green juice was. Tell me what happened when you called your best friend.

_____

_____

_____

_____

_____

_____

_____

_____

_____

_____

_____

_____

_____

_____

_____

_____

_____

_____

_____

_____

_____

_____

_____

_____

_____

_____

_____

_____

_____

_____

Real Date: _____

STEP 2: SPEND WITHOUT WORRY ☀

Everyday journal what you purchased with a pretend $1,000. You can't save any money for the next day, you must use it in the day it is given. Everyday increase the amount by multiplying the amount from the day before by 2.

_____

_____

_____

_____

_____

_____

_____

_____

Total Purchased Today: $_____

Step 3: Receive ☻

"Everything that is in this journal, shall come to be."

Tell me if you see evidence of your pretend life in your real life. Be grateful and notice even the smallest evidence of the law of attraction. The more you are grateful and paying attention, the faster your desires will manifests.

"I have evidence of my abundance in my real life."

Real Date: _____

_____

_____

_____

_____

_____

_____

_____

_____

_____

_____

_____

STEP 1: PLAY PRETEND

Journal your entire day in great detail. Tell me how good your green juice was. Tell me what happened when you called your best friend.

_____
_____
_____
_____
_____
_____
_____
_____
_____
_____
_____
_____
_____
_____
_____
_____
_____
_____
_____
_____
_____
_____
_____
_____
_____
_____
_____
_____
_____
_____
_____
_____

Real Date: _____

STEP 2: SPEND WITHOUT WORRY ☼

Everyday journal what you purchased with a pretend $1,000. You can't save any money for the next day, you must use it in the day it is given. Everyday increase the amount by multiplying the amount from the day before by 2.

_____

_____

_____

_____

_____

_____

_____

_____

Total Purchased Today: $_____

Step 3: Receive ☼

"Everything that is in this journal, shall come to be."

Tell me if you see evidence of your pretend life in your real life. Be grateful and notice even the smallest evidence of the law of attraction. The more you are grateful and paying attention, the faster your desires will manifests.

"I have evidence of my abundance in my real life."

Real Date: _____

_____

_____

_____

_____

_____

_____

_____

_____

_____

_____

_____

_____

STEP 1: PLAY PRETEND

Journal your entire day in great detail. Tell me how good your green juice was. Tell me what happened when you called your best friend.

_____
_____
_____
_____
_____
_____
_____
_____
_____
_____
_____
_____
_____
_____
_____
_____
_____
_____
_____
_____
_____
_____
_____
_____
_____
_____
_____
_____
_____
_____
_____
_____

Real Date: _____

STEP 2: SPEND WITHOUT WORRY ☀

Everyday journal what you purchased with a pretend $1,000. You can't save any money for the next day, you must use it in the day it is given. Everyday increase the amount by multiplying the amount from the day before by 2.

_____
_____
_____
_____
_____
_____
_____
_____

Total Purchased Today: $_____

Step 3: Receive ☺

"Everything that is in this journal, shall come to be."

Tell me if you see evidence of your pretend life in your real life. Be grateful and notice even the smallest evidence of the law of attraction. The more you are grateful and paying attention, the faster your desires will manifests.

"I have evidence of my abundance in my real life."

Real Date: _____

_____
_____
_____
_____
_____
_____
_____
_____
_____
_____
_____

STEP 1: PLAY PRETEND

Journal your entire day in great detail. Tell me how good your green juice was. Tell me what happened when you called your best friend.

_____
_____
_____
_____
_____
_____
_____
_____
_____
_____
_____
_____
_____
_____
_____
_____
_____
_____
_____
_____
_____
_____
_____
_____
_____
_____
_____
_____
_____
_____

Real Date: _____

STEP 2: SPEND WITHOUT WORRY ☼

Everyday journal what you purchased with a pretend $1,000. You can't save any money for the next day, you must use it in the day it is given. Everyday increase the amount by multiplying the amount from the day before by 2.

_____
_____
_____
_____
_____
_____
_____
_____
_____

Total Purchased Today: $_____

Step 3: Receive ☺

"Everything that is in this journal, shall come to be."
Tell me if you see evidence of your pretend life in your real life. Be grateful and notice even the smallest evidence of the law of attraction. The more you are grateful and paying attention, the faster your desires will manifests.

"I have evidence of my abundance in my real life."

Real Date: _____

_____
_____
_____
_____
_____
_____
_____
_____
_____
_____
_____

STEP 1: PLAY PRETEND

Journal your entire day in great detail. Tell me how good your green juice was. Tell me what happened when you called your best friend.

_____

_____

_____

_____

_____

_____

_____

_____

_____

_____

_____

_____

_____

_____

_____

_____

_____

_____

_____

_____

_____

_____

_____

_____

_____

_____

_____

_____

_____

Real Date: _____

STEP 2: SPEND WITHOUT WORRY ☀

Everyday journal what you purchased with a pretend $1,000. You can't save any money for the next day, you must use it in the day it is given. Everyday increase the amount by multiplying the amount from the day before by 2.

_____

_____

_____

_____

_____

_____

_____

_____

Total Purchased Today: $_____

Step 3: Receive ☀

"Everything that is in this journal, shall come to be."

Tell me if you see evidence of your pretend life in your real life. Be grateful and notice even the smallest evidence of the law of attraction. The more you are grateful and paying attention, the faster your desires will manifests.

"I have evidence of my abundance in my real life."

Real Date: _____

_____

_____

_____

_____

_____

_____

_____

_____

_____

_____

STEP 1: PLAY PRETEND

Journal your entire day in great detail. Tell me how good your green juice was. Tell me what happened when you called your best friend.

_____
_____
_____
_____
_____
_____
_____
_____
_____
_____
_____
_____
_____
_____
_____
_____
_____
_____
_____
_____
_____
_____
_____
_____
_____
_____
_____
_____
_____

Real Date: _____

STEP 2: SPEND WITHOUT WORRY ☀

Everyday journal what you purchased with a pretend $1,000. You can't save any money for the next day, you must use it in the day it is given. Everyday increase the amount by multiplying the amount from the day before by 2.

_____

_____

_____

_____

_____

_____

_____

_____

Total Purchased Today: $_____

Step 3: Receive ☺

"Everything that is in this journal, shall come to be."

Tell me if you see evidence of your pretend life in your real life. Be grateful and notice even the smallest evidence of the law of attraction. The more you are grateful and paying attention, the faster your desires will manifests.

"I have evidence of my abundance in my real life."

Real Date: _____

_____

_____

_____

_____

_____

_____

_____

_____

_____

_____

_____

STEP 1: PLAY PRETEND

Journal your entire day in great detail. Tell me how good your green juice was. Tell me what happened when you called your best friend.

_____
_____
_____
_____
_____
_____
_____
_____
_____
_____
_____
_____
_____
_____
_____
_____
_____
_____
_____
_____
_____
_____
_____
_____
_____
_____
_____
_____
_____
_____

Real Date: _____

STEP 2: SPEND WITHOUT WORRY ☼

Everyday journal what you purchased with a pretend $1,000. You can't save any money for the next day, you must use it in the day it is given. Everyday increase the amount by multiplying the amount from the day before by 2.

_____

_____

_____

_____

_____

_____

_____

_____

Total Purchased Today: $_____

Step 3: Receive ☼

"Everything that is in this journal, shall come to be."

Tell me if you see evidence of your pretend life in your real life. Be grateful and notice even the smallest evidence of the law of attraction. The more you are grateful and paying attention, the faster your desires will manifests.

"I have evidence of my abundance in my real life."

Real Date: _____

_____

_____

_____

_____

_____

_____

_____

_____

_____

_____

STEP 1: PLAY PRETEND

Journal your entire day in great detail. Tell me how good your green juice was. Tell me what happened when you called your best friend.

_____
_____
_____
_____
_____
_____
_____
_____
_____
_____
_____
_____
_____
_____
_____
_____
_____
_____
_____
_____
_____
_____
_____
_____
_____
_____
_____
_____
_____

Real Date: _____

STEP 2: SPEND WITHOUT WORRY ☼

Everyday journal what you purchased with a pretend $1,000. You can't save any money for the next day, you must use it in the day it is given. Everyday increase the amount by multiplying the amount from the day before by 2.

_____
_____
_____
_____
_____
_____
_____
_____

_____

Total Purchased Today: $_____

Step 3: Receive ☼

"Everything that is in this journal, shall come to be."

Tell me if you see evidence of your pretend life in your real life. Be grateful and notice even the smallest evidence of the law of attraction. The more you are grateful and paying attention, the faster your desires will manifests.

"I have evidence of my abundance in my real life."

Real Date: _____

_____
_____
_____
_____
_____
_____
_____
_____
_____
_____
_____

STEP 1: PLAY PRETEND

Journal your entire day in great detail. Tell me how good your green juice was. Tell me what happened when you called your best friend.

_____

_____

_____

_____

_____

_____

_____

_____

_____

_____

_____

_____

_____

_____

_____

_____

_____

_____

_____

_____

_____

_____

_____

_____

_____

_____

_____

_____

Real Date: _____

STEP 2: SPEND WITHOUT WORRY ☀

Everyday journal what you purchased with a pretend $1,000. You can't save any money for the next day, you must use it in the day it is given. Everyday increase the amount by multiplying the amount from the day before by 2.

_____
_____
_____
_____
_____
_____
_____
_____
_____

Total Purchased Today: $_____

Step 3: Receive ☀

"Everything that is in this journal, shall come to be."

Tell me if you see evidence of your pretend life in your real life. Be grateful and notice even the smallest evidence of the law of attraction. The more you are grateful and paying attention, the faster your desires will manifests.

"I have evidence of my abundance in my real life."

Real Date: _____

_____
_____
_____
_____
_____
_____
_____
_____
_____
_____
_____

STEP 1: PLAY PRETEND

Journal your entire day in great detail. Tell me how good your green juice was. Tell me what happened when you called your best friend.

_____

_____

_____

_____

_____

_____

_____

_____

_____

_____

_____

_____

_____

_____

_____

_____

_____

_____

_____

_____

_____

_____

_____

_____

_____

_____

_____

_____

_____

_____

_____

_____

_____

_____

Real Date: _____

STEP 2: SPEND WITHOUT WORRY ☀

Everyday journal what you purchased with a pretend $1,000. You can't save any money for the next day, you must use it in the day it is given. Everyday increase the amount by multiplying the amount from the day before by 2.

_____
_____
_____
_____
_____
_____
_____
_____
_____

Total Purchased Today: $_____

Step 3: Receive ☺

"Everything that is in this journal, shall come to be."

Tell me if you see evidence of your pretend life in your real life. Be grateful and notice even the smallest evidence of the law of attraction. The more you are grateful and paying attention, the faster your desires will manifests.

"I have evidence of my abundance in my real life."

Real Date: _____

_____
_____
_____
_____
_____
_____
_____
_____
_____
_____
_____
_____

STEP 1: PLAY PRETEND

Journal your entire day in great detail. Tell me how good your green juice was. Tell me what happened when you called your best friend.

_____
_____
_____
_____
_____
_____
_____
_____
_____
_____
_____
_____
_____
_____
_____
_____
_____
_____
_____
_____
_____
_____
_____
_____
_____
_____
_____
_____
_____
_____

Real Date: _____

STEP 2: SPEND WITHOUT WORRY ☀

Everyday journal what you purchased with a pretend $1,000. You can't save any money for the next day, you must use it in the day it is given. Everyday increase the amount by multiplying the amount from the day before by 2.

_____

_____

_____

_____

_____

_____

_____

Total Purchased Today: $_____

Step 3: Receive ☀

"Everything that is in this journal, shall come to be."

Tell me if you see evidence of your pretend life in your real life. Be grateful and notice even the smallest evidence of the law of attraction. The more you are grateful and paying attention, the faster your desires will manifests.

"I have evidence of my abundance in my real life."

Real Date: _____

_____

_____

_____

_____

_____

_____

_____

_____

_____

STEP 1: PLAY PRETEND

Journal your entire day in great detail. Tell me how good your green juice was. Tell me what happened when you called your best friend.

_____

_____

_____

_____

_____

_____

_____

_____

_____

_____

_____

_____

_____

_____

_____

_____

_____

_____

_____

_____

_____

_____

_____

_____

_____

_____

_____

_____

_____

_____

Real Date: _____

STEP 2: SPEND WITHOUT WORRY ☀

Everyday journal what you purchased with a pretend $1,000. You can't save any money for the next day, you must use it in the day it is given. Everyday increase the amount by multiplying the amount from the day before by 2.

_____

_____

_____

_____

_____

_____

_____

_____

_____

Total Purchased Today: $_____

Step 3: Receive ☺

"Everything that is in this journal, shall come to be."
Tell me if you see evidence of your pretend life in your real life. Be grateful and notice even the smallest evidence of the law of attraction. The more you are grateful and paying attention, the faster your desires will manifests.

"I have evidence of my abundance in my real life."

Real Date: _____

_____

_____

_____

_____

_____

_____

_____

_____

_____

_____

_____

STEP 1: PLAY PRETEND

Journal your entire day in great detail. Tell me how good your green juice was. Tell me what happened when you called your best friend.

_____

_____

_____

_____

_____

_____

_____

_____

_____

_____

_____

_____

_____

_____

_____

_____

_____

_____

_____

_____

_____

_____

_____

_____

_____

Real Date: _____

STEP 2: SPEND WITHOUT WORRY ☼

Everyday journal what you purchased with a pretend $1,000. You can't save any money for the next day, you must use it in the day it is given. Everyday increase the amount by multiplying the amount from the day before by 2.

_____

_____

_____

_____

_____

_____

_____

_____

_____

Total Purchased Today: $_____

Step 3: Receive ☺

"Everything that is in this journal, shall come to be."

Tell me if you see evidence of your pretend life in your real life. Be grateful and notice even the smallest evidence of the law of attraction. The more you are grateful and paying attention, the faster your desires will manifests.

"I have evidence of my abundance in my real life."

Real Date: _____

_____

_____

_____

_____

_____

_____

_____

_____

_____

_____

_____

STEP 1: PLAY PRETEND

Journal your entire day in great detail. Tell me how good your green juice was. Tell me what happened when you called your best friend.

_____
_____
_____
_____
_____
_____
_____
_____
_____
_____
_____
_____
_____
_____
_____
_____
_____
_____
_____
_____
_____
_____
_____
_____
_____
_____
_____
_____

Real Date: _____

STEP 2: SPEND WITHOUT WORRY ☀

Everyday journal what you purchased with a pretend $1,000. You can't save any money for the next day, you must use it in the day it is given. Everyday increase the amount by multiplying the amount from the day before by 2.

_____

_____

_____

_____

_____

_____

_____

_____

Total Purchased Today: $_____

Step 3: Receive ☺

"Everything that is in this journal, shall come to be."

Tell me if you see evidence of your pretend life in your real life. Be grateful and notice even the smallest evidence of the law of attraction. The more you are grateful and paying attention, the faster your desires will manifests.

"I have evidence of my abundance in my real life."

Real Date: _____

_____

_____

_____

_____

_____

_____

_____

_____

_____

_____

STEP 1: PLAY PRETEND 🐝

Journal your entire day in great detail. Tell me how good your green juice was. Tell me what happened when you called your best friend.

_____
_____
_____
_____
_____
_____
_____
_____
_____
_____
_____
_____
_____
_____
_____
_____
_____
_____
_____
_____
_____
_____
_____
_____
_____
_____
_____
_____
_____

Real Date: _____

STEP 2: SPEND WITHOUT WORRY ☼

Everyday journal what you purchased with a pretend $1,000. You can't save any money for the next day, you must use it in the day it is given. Everyday increase the amount by multiplying the amount from the day before by 2.

_____

_____

_____

_____

_____

_____

_____

_____

Total Purchased Today: $_____

Step 3: Receive ☼

"Everything that is in this journal, shall come to be."

Tell me if you see evidence of your pretend life in your real life. Be grateful and notice even the smallest evidence of the law of attraction. The more you are grateful and paying attention, the faster your desires will manifests.

"I have evidence of my abundance in my real life."

Real Date: _____

_____

_____

_____

_____

_____

_____

_____

_____

_____

_____

_____

STEP 1: PLAY PRETEND

Journal your entire day in great detail. Tell me how good your green juice was. Tell me what happened when you called your best friend.

_____
_____
_____
_____
_____
_____
_____
_____
_____
_____
_____
_____
_____
_____
_____
_____
_____
_____
_____
_____
_____
_____
_____
_____
_____
_____
_____

Real Date: _____

STEP 2: SPEND WITHOUT WORRY ☀

Everyday journal what you purchased with a pretend $1,000. You can't save any money for the next day, you must use it in the day it is given. Everyday increase the amount by multiplying the amount from the day before by 2.

_____

_____

_____

_____

_____

_____

_____

_____

Total Purchased Today: $_____

Step 3: Receive ☀

"Everything that is in this journal, shall come to be."

Tell me if you see evidence of your pretend life in your real life. Be grateful and notice even the smallest evidence of the law of attraction. The more you are grateful and paying attention, the faster your desires will manifests.

"I have evidence of my abundance in my real life."

Real Date: _____

_____

_____

_____

_____

_____

_____

_____

_____

_____

_____

_____

STEP 1: PLAY PRETEND

Journal your entire day in great detail. Tell me how good your green juice was. Tell me what happened when you called your best friend.

_____

_____

_____

_____

_____

_____

_____

_____

_____

_____

_____

_____

_____

_____

_____

_____

_____

_____

_____

_____

_____

_____

_____

_____

_____

_____

_____

_____

_____

_____

Real Date: _____

STEP 2: SPEND WITHOUT WORRY ☀

Everyday journal what you purchased with a pretend $1,000. You can't save any money for the next day, you must use it in the day it is given. Everyday increase the amount by multiplying the amount from the day before by 2.

_____

_____

_____

_____

_____

_____

_____

_____

_____

Total Purchased Today: $_____

Step 3: Receive ☺

"Everything that is in this journal, shall come to be."

Tell me if you see evidence of your pretend life in your real life. Be grateful and notice even the smallest evidence of the law of attraction. The more you are grateful and paying attention, the faster your desires will manifests.

"I have evidence of my abundance in my real life."

Real Date: _____

_____

_____

_____

_____

_____

_____

_____

_____

_____

_____

_____

STEP 1: PLAY PRETEND

Journal your entire day in great detail. Tell me how good your green juice was. Tell me what happened when you called your best friend.

_____
_____
_____
_____
_____
_____
_____
_____
_____
_____
_____
_____
_____
_____
_____
_____
_____
_____
_____
_____
_____
_____
_____
_____
_____
_____
_____
_____
_____

Real Date: _____

STEP 2: SPEND WITHOUT WORRY ☼

Everyday journal what you purchased with a pretend $1,000. You can't save any money for the next day, you must use it in the day it is given. Everyday increase the amount by multiplying the amount from the day before by 2.

_____

_____

_____

_____

_____

_____

_____

_____

_____

Total Purchased Today: $_____

Step 3: Receive ☼

"Everything that is in this journal, shall come to be."

Tell me if you see evidence of your pretend life in your real life. Be grateful and notice even the smallest evidence of the law of attraction. The more you are grateful and paying attention, the faster your desires will manifests.

"I have evidence of my abundance in my real life."

Real Date: _____

_____

_____

_____

_____

_____

_____

_____

_____

_____

_____

STEP 1: PLAY PRETEND

Journal your entire day in great detail. Tell me how good your green juice was. Tell me what happened when you called your best friend.

_____
_____
_____
_____
_____
_____
_____
_____
_____
_____
_____
_____
_____
_____
_____
_____
_____
_____
_____
_____
_____
_____
_____
_____
_____
_____
_____
_____
_____

Real Date: _____

STEP 2: SPEND WITHOUT WORRY ☼

Everyday journal what you purchased with a pretend $1,000. You can't save any money for the next day, you must use it in the day it is given. Everyday increase the amount by multiplying the amount from the day before by 2.

_____

_____

_____

_____

_____

_____

_____

_____

Total Purchased Today: $_____

Step 3: Receive ☼

"Everything that is in this journal, shall come to be."

Tell me if you see evidence of your pretend life in your real life. Be grateful and notice even the smallest evidence of the law of attraction. The more you are grateful and paying attention, the faster your desires will manifests.

"I have evidence of my abundance in my real life."

Real Date: _____

_____

_____

_____

_____

_____

_____

_____

_____

_____

_____

_____

STEP 1: PLAY PRETEND

Journal your entire day in great detail. Tell me how good your green juice was. Tell me what happened when you called your best friend.

_____
_____
_____
_____
_____
_____
_____
_____
_____
_____
_____
_____
_____
_____
_____
_____
_____
_____
_____
_____
_____
_____
_____
_____
_____
_____
_____
_____
_____
_____
_____

Real Date: _____

STEP 2: SPEND WITHOUT WORRY ☼

Everyday journal what you purchased with a pretend $1,000. You can't save any money for the next day, you must use it in the day it is given. Everyday increase the amount by multiplying the amount from the day before by 2.

_____

_____

_____

_____

_____

_____

_____

_____

_____

Total Purchased Today: $_____

Step 3: Receive ☼

"Everything that is in this journal, shall come to be."

Tell me if you see evidence of your pretend life in your real life. Be grateful and notice even the smallest evidence of the law of attraction. The more you are grateful and paying attention, the faster your desires will manifests.

"I have evidence of my abundance in my real life."

Real Date: _____

_____

_____

_____

_____

_____

_____

_____

_____

_____

_____

_____

STEP 1: PLAY PRETEND

Journal your entire day in great detail. Tell me how good your green juice was. Tell me what happened when you called your best friend.

_____

_____

_____

_____

_____

_____

_____

_____

_____

_____

_____

_____

_____

_____

_____

_____

_____

_____

_____

_____

_____

_____

_____

_____

Real Date: _____

STEP 2: SPEND WITHOUT WORRY ☼

Everyday journal what you purchased with a pretend $1,000. You can't save any money for the next day, you must use it in the day it is given. Everyday increase the amount by multiplying the amount from the day before by 2.

_____
_____
_____
_____
_____
_____
_____
_____
_____

Total Purchased Today: $_____

Step 3: Receive ☼

"Everything that is in this journal, shall come to be."
Tell me if you see evidence of your pretend life in your real life. Be grateful and notice even the smallest evidence of the law of attraction. The more you are grateful and paying attention, the faster your desires will manifests.

"I have evidence of my abundance in my real life."

Real Date: _____

_____
_____
_____
_____
_____
_____
_____
_____
_____
_____
_____

STEP 1: PLAY PRETEND

Journal your entire day in great detail. Tell me how good your green juice was. Tell me what happened when you called your best friend.

Real Date: _____

STEP 2: SPEND WITHOUT WORRY ☀

Everyday journal what you purchased with a pretend $1,000. You can't save any money for the next day, you must use it in the day it is given. Everyday increase the amount by multiplying the amount from the day before by 2.

_____

_____

_____

_____

_____

_____

_____

_____

Total Purchased Today: $_____

Step 3: Receive ☀

"Everything that is in this journal, shall come to be."

Tell me if you see evidence of your pretend life in your real life. Be grateful and notice even the smallest evidence of the law of attraction. The more you are grateful and paying attention, the faster your desires will manifests.

"I have evidence of my abundance in my real life."

Real Date: _____

_____

_____

_____

_____

_____

_____

_____

_____

_____

_____

_____

STEP 1: PLAY PRETEND 🐝

Journal your entire day in great detail. Tell me how good your green juice was. Tell me what happened when you called your best friend.

_____

_____

_____

_____

_____

_____

_____

_____

_____

_____

_____

_____

_____

_____

_____

_____

_____

_____

_____

_____

_____

_____

_____

_____

_____

_____

_____

_____

_____

_____

Real Date: _____

STEP 2: SPEND WITHOUT WORRY ☼

Everyday journal what you purchased with a pretend $1,000. You can't save any money for the next day, you must use it in the day it is given. Everyday increase the amount by multiplying the amount from the day before by 2.

_____
_____
_____
_____
_____
_____
_____
_____

Total Purchased Today: $_____

Step 3: Receive ☼

"Everything that is in this journal, shall come to be."

Tell me if you see evidence of your pretend life in your real life. Be grateful and notice even the smallest evidence of the law of attraction. The more you are grateful and paying attention, the faster your desires will manifests.

"I have evidence of my abundance in my real life."

Real Date: _____

_____
_____
_____
_____
_____
_____
_____
_____
_____
_____
_____

STEP 1: PLAY PRETEND

Journal your entire day in great detail. Tell me how good your green juice was. Tell me what happened when you called your best friend.

_____

_____

_____

_____

_____

_____

_____

_____

_____

_____

_____

_____

_____

_____

_____

_____

_____

_____

_____

_____

_____

_____

_____

_____

_____

_____

_____

_____

_____

_____

_____

_____

_____

_____

Real Date: _____

STEP 2: SPEND WITHOUT WORRY ☀

Everyday journal what you purchased with a pretend $1,000. You can't save any money for the next day, you must use it in the day it is given. Everyday increase the amount by multiplying the amount from the day before by 2.

_____

_____

_____

_____

_____

_____

_____

_____

_____

Total Purchased Today: $_____

Step 3: Receive ☺

"Everything that is in this journal, shall come to be."
Tell me if you see evidence of your pretend life in your real life. Be grateful and notice even the smallest evidence of the law of attraction. The more you are grateful and paying attention, the faster your desires will manifests.

"I have evidence of my abundance in my real life."

Real Date: _____

_____

_____

_____

_____

_____

_____

_____

_____

_____

_____

_____

STEP 1: PLAY PRETEND 🐝

Journal your entire day in great detail. Tell me how good your green juice was. Tell me what happened when you called your best friend.

_____

_____

_____

_____

_____

_____

_____

_____

_____

_____

_____

_____

_____

_____

_____

_____

_____

_____

_____

_____

_____

_____

_____

_____

_____

_____

_____

_____

_____

_____

Real Date: _____

STEP 2: SPEND WITHOUT WORRY ☼

Everyday journal what you purchased with a pretend $1,000. You can't save any money for the next day, you must use it in the day it is given. Everyday increase the amount by multiplying the amount from the day before by 2.

_____
_____
_____
_____
_____
_____
_____
_____
_____

Total Purchased Today: $_____

Step 3: Receive ☼

"Everything that is in this journal, shall come to be."

Tell me if you see evidence of your pretend life in your real life. Be grateful and notice even the smallest evidence of the law of attraction. The more you are grateful and paying attention, the faster your desires will manifests.

"I have evidence of my abundance in my real life."

Real Date: _____

_____
_____
_____
_____
_____
_____
_____
_____
_____
_____
_____

STEP 1: PLAY PRETEND

Journal your entire day in great detail. Tell me how good your green juice was. Tell me what happened when you called your best friend.

_____

_____

_____

_____

_____

_____

_____

_____

_____

_____

_____

_____

_____

_____

_____

_____

_____

_____

_____

_____

_____

_____

_____

_____

_____

_____

_____

_____

_____

_____

Real Date: _____

PLAYING PRETEND – LAW OF ATTRACTION PLANNER

STEP 2: SPEND WITHOUT WORRY ☼

Everyday journal what you purchased with a pretend $1,000. You can't save any money for the next day, you must use it in the day it is given. Everyday increase the amount by multiplying the amount from the day before by 2.

_____

_____

_____

_____

_____

_____

_____

_____

Total Purchased Today: $_____

Step 3: Receive ☺

"Everything that is in this journal, shall come to be."

Tell me if you see evidence of your pretend life in your real life. Be grateful and notice even the smallest evidence of the law of attraction. The more you are grateful and paying attention, the faster your desires will manifests.

"I have evidence of my abundance in my real life."

Real Date: _____

_____

_____

_____

_____

_____

_____

_____

_____

_____

_____

_____

STEP 1: PLAY PRETEND

Journal your entire day in great detail. Tell me how good your green juice was. Tell me what happened when you called your best friend.

_____

_____

_____

_____

_____

_____

_____

_____

_____

_____

_____

_____

_____

_____

_____

_____

_____

_____

_____

_____

_____

_____

_____

_____

_____

_____

_____

Real Date: _____

STEP 2: SPEND WITHOUT WORRY ☼

Everyday journal what you purchased with a pretend $1,000. You can't save any money for the next day, you must use it in the day it is given. Everyday increase the amount by multiplying the amount from the day before by 2.

_____
_____
_____
_____
_____
_____
_____
_____
_____

Total Purchased Today: $_____

Step 3: Receive ☼

"Everything that is in this journal, shall come to be."

Tell me if you see evidence of your pretend life in your real life. Be grateful and notice even the smallest evidence of the law of attraction. The more you are grateful and paying attention, the faster your desires will manifests.

"I have evidence of my abundance in my real life."

Real Date: _____

_____
_____
_____
_____
_____
_____
_____
_____
_____
_____
_____

STEP 1: PLAY PRETEND 🐝

Journal your entire day in great detail. Tell me how good your green juice was. Tell me what happened when you called your best friend.

_____
_____
_____
_____
_____
_____
_____
_____
_____
_____
_____
_____
_____
_____
_____
_____
_____
_____
_____
_____
_____
_____
_____
_____
_____
_____
_____
_____
_____
_____
_____

Real Date: _____

STEP 2: SPEND WITHOUT WORRY ☀

Everyday journal what you purchased with a pretend $1,000. You can't save any money for the next day, you must use it in the day it is given. Everyday increase the amount by multiplying the amount from the day before by 2.

_____
_____
_____
_____
_____
_____
_____
_____

Total Purchased Today: $_____

Step 3: Receive ☺

"Everything that is in this journal, shall come to be."

Tell me if you see evidence of your pretend life in your real life. Be grateful and notice even the smallest evidence of the law of attraction. The more you are grateful and paying attention, the faster your desires will manifests.

"I have evidence of my abundance in my real life."

Real Date: _____

_____
_____
_____
_____
_____
_____
_____
_____
_____
_____
_____

STEP 1: PLAY PRETEND

Journal your entire day in great detail. Tell me how good your green juice was. Tell me what happened when you called your best friend.

_____

_____

_____

_____

_____

_____

_____

_____

_____

_____

_____

_____

_____

_____

_____

_____

_____

_____

_____

_____

_____

_____

_____

_____

_____

_____

_____

_____

_____

_____

Real Date: _____

STEP 2: SPEND WITHOUT WORRY ☼

Everyday journal what you purchased with a pretend $1,000. You can't save any money for the next day, you must use it in the day it is given. Everyday increase the amount by multiplying the amount from the day before by 2.

_____
_____
_____
_____
_____
_____
_____
_____
_____

Total Purchased Today: $_____

Step 3: Receive ☼

"Everything that is in this journal, shall come to be."

Tell me if you see evidence of your pretend life in your real life. Be grateful and notice even the smallest evidence of the law of attraction. The more you are grateful and paying attention, the faster your desires will manifests.

"I have evidence of my abundance in my real life."

Real Date: _____

_____
_____
_____
_____
_____
_____
_____
_____
_____
_____
_____

STEP 1: PLAY PRETEND

Journal your entire day in great detail. Tell me how good your green juice was. Tell me what happened when you called your best friend.

_____

_____

_____

_____

_____

_____

_____

_____

_____

_____

_____

_____

_____

_____

_____

_____

_____

_____

_____

_____

_____

_____

_____

_____

_____

_____

_____

_____

Real Date: _____

STEP 2: SPEND WITHOUT WORRY ☼

Everyday journal what you purchased with a pretend $1,000. You can't save any money for the next day, you must use it in the day it is given. Everyday increase the amount by multiplying the amount from the day before by 2.

_____

_____

_____

_____

_____

_____

_____

_____

_____

Total Purchased Today: $_____

Step 3: Receive ☼

"Everything that is in this journal, shall come to be."

Tell me if you see evidence of your pretend life in your real life. Be grateful and notice even the smallest evidence of the law of attraction. The more you are grateful and paying attention, the faster your desires will manifests.

"I have evidence of my abundance in my real life."

Real Date: _____

_____

_____

_____

_____

_____

_____

_____

_____

_____

_____

_____

STEP 1: PLAY PRETEND

Journal your entire day in great detail. Tell me how good your green juice was. Tell me what happened when you called your best friend.

_____
_____
_____
_____
_____
_____
_____
_____
_____
_____
_____
_____
_____
_____
_____
_____
_____
_____
_____
_____
_____
_____
_____
_____
_____
_____
_____
_____
_____
_____
_____

Real Date: _____

STEP 2: SPEND WITHOUT WORRY ☀

Everyday journal what you purchased with a pretend $1,000. You can't save any money for the next day, you must use it in the day it is given. Everyday increase the amount by multiplying the amount from the day before by 2.

_____

_____

_____

_____

_____

_____

_____

_____

Total Purchased Today: $_____

Step 3: Receive ☀

"Everything that is in this journal, shall come to be."
Tell me if you see evidence of your pretend life in your real life. Be grateful and notice even the smallest evidence of the law of attraction. The more you are grateful and paying attention, the faster your desires will manifests.

"I have evidence of my abundance in my real life."

Real Date: _____

_____

_____

_____

_____

_____

_____

_____

_____

_____

_____

_____

STEP 1: PLAY PRETEND

Journal your entire day in great detail. Tell me how good your green juice was. Tell me what happened when you called your best friend.

_____
_____
_____
_____
_____
_____
_____
_____
_____
_____
_____
_____
_____
_____
_____
_____
_____
_____
_____
_____
_____
_____
_____
_____
_____
_____
_____
_____
_____

Real Date: _____

STEP 2: SPEND WITHOUT WORRY ☼

Everyday journal what you purchased with a pretend $1,000. You can't save any money for the next day, you must use it in the day it is given. Everyday increase the amount by multiplying the amount from the day before by 2.

_____
_____
_____
_____
_____
_____
_____
_____

Total Purchased Today: $_____

Step 3: Receive ☼

"Everything that is in this journal, shall come to be."

Tell me if you see evidence of your pretend life in your real life. Be grateful and notice even the smallest evidence of the law of attraction. The more you are grateful and paying attention, the faster your desires will manifests.

"I have evidence of my abundance in my real life."

Real Date: _____

_____
_____
_____
_____
_____
_____
_____
_____
_____
_____
_____

STEP 1: PLAY PRETEND 🐝

Journal your entire day in great detail. Tell me how good your green juice was. Tell me what happened when you called your best friend.

_____

_____

_____

_____

_____

_____

_____

_____

_____

_____

_____

_____

_____

_____

_____

_____

_____

_____

_____

_____

_____

_____

_____

_____

_____

_____

_____

_____

_____

_____

Real Date: _____

STEP 2: SPEND WITHOUT WORRY ☀

Everyday journal what you purchased with a pretend $1,000. You can't save any money for the next day, you must use it in the day it is given. Everyday increase the amount by multiplying the amount from the day before by 2.

_____

_____

_____

_____

_____

_____

_____

_____

Total Purchased Today: $_____

Step 3: Receive ☀

"Everything that is in this journal, shall come to be."

Tell me if you see evidence of your pretend life in your real life. Be grateful and notice even the smallest evidence of the law of attraction. The more you are grateful and paying attention, the faster your desires will manifests.

"I have evidence of my abundance in my real life."

Real Date: _____

_____

_____

_____

_____

_____

_____

_____

_____

_____

_____

_____

STEP 1: PLAY PRETEND

Journal your entire day in great detail. Tell me how good your green juice was. Tell me what happened when you called your best friend.

_____
_____
_____
_____
_____
_____
_____
_____
_____
_____
_____
_____
_____
_____
_____
_____
_____
_____
_____
_____
_____
_____
_____
_____
_____
_____
_____
_____

Real Date: _____

STEP 2: SPEND WITHOUT WORRY ☀

Everyday journal what you purchased with a pretend $1,000. You can't save any money for the next day, you must use it in the day it is given. Everyday increase the amount by multiplying the amount from the day before by 2.

_____

_____

_____

_____

_____

_____

_____

_____

Total Purchased Today: $_____

Step 3: Receive ☀

"Everything that is in this journal, shall come to be."

Tell me if you see evidence of your pretend life in your real life. Be grateful and notice even the smallest evidence of the law of attraction. The more you are grateful and paying attention, the faster your desires will manifests.

"I have evidence of my abundance in my real life."

Real Date: _____

_____

_____

_____

_____

_____

_____

_____

_____

_____

_____

_____

STEP 1: PLAY PRETEND

Journal your entire day in great detail. Tell me how good your green juice was. Tell me what happened when you called your best friend.

_____
_____
_____
_____
_____
_____
_____
_____
_____
_____
_____
_____
_____
_____
_____
_____
_____
_____
_____
_____
_____
_____
_____
_____
_____
_____
_____
_____
_____

Real Date: _____

STEP 2: SPEND WITHOUT WORRY ☼

Everyday journal what you purchased with a pretend $1,000. You can't save any money for the next day, you must use it in the day it is given. Everyday increase the amount by multiplying the amount from the day before by 2.

_____
_____
_____
_____
_____
_____
_____
_____

_____

Total Purchased Today: $_____

Step 3: Receive ☼

"Everything that is in this journal, shall come to be."

Tell me if you see evidence of your pretend life in your real life. Be grateful and notice even the smallest evidence of the law of attraction. The more you are grateful and paying attention, the faster your desires will manifests.

"I have evidence of my abundance in my real life."

Real Date: _____

_____
_____
_____
_____
_____
_____
_____
_____
_____
_____
_____

STEP 1: PLAY PRETEND

Journal your entire day in great detail. Tell me how good your green juice was. Tell me what happened when you called your best friend.

_____
_____
_____
_____
_____
_____
_____
_____
_____
_____
_____
_____
_____
_____
_____
_____
_____
_____
_____
_____
_____
_____
_____
_____
_____
_____
_____
_____
_____
_____

Real Date: _____

STEP 2: SPEND WITHOUT WORRY ☀

Everyday journal what you purchased with a pretend $1,000. You can't save any money for the next day, you must use it in the day it is given. Everyday increase the amount by multiplying the amount from the day before by 2.

_____
_____
_____
_____
_____
_____
_____
_____

_____

Total Purchased Today: $_____

Step 3: Receive ☀

"Everything that is in this journal, shall come to be."
Tell me if you see evidence of your pretend life in your real life. Be grateful and notice even the smallest evidence of the law of attraction. The more you are grateful and paying attention, the faster your desires will manifests.

"I have evidence of my abundance in my real life."

Real Date: _____

_____
_____
_____
_____
_____
_____
_____
_____
_____
_____
_____

STEP 1: PLAY PRETEND

Journal your entire day in great detail. Tell me how good your green juice was. Tell me what happened when you called your best friend.

_____

_____

_____

_____

_____

_____

_____

_____

_____

_____

_____

_____

_____

_____

_____

_____

_____

_____

_____

_____

_____

_____

_____

_____

_____

Real Date: _____

STEP 2: SPEND WITHOUT WORRY ☀

Everyday journal what you purchased with a pretend $1,000. You can't save any money for the next day, you must use it in the day it is given. Everyday increase the amount by multiplying the amount from the day before by 2.

_____
_____
_____
_____
_____
_____
_____
_____

Total Purchased Today: $_____

Step 3: Receive ☀

"Everything that is in this journal, shall come to be."
Tell me if you see evidence of your pretend life in your real life. Be grateful and notice even the smallest evidence of the law of attraction. The more you are grateful and paying attention, the faster your desires will manifests.

"I have evidence of my abundance in my real life."

Real Date: _____

_____
_____
_____
_____
_____
_____
_____
_____
_____
_____
_____

STEP 1: PLAY PRETEND

Journal your entire day in great detail. Tell me how good your green juice was. Tell me what happened when you called your best friend.

_____
_____
_____
_____
_____
_____
_____
_____
_____
_____
_____
_____
_____
_____
_____
_____
_____
_____
_____
_____
_____
_____
_____
_____
_____
_____
_____
_____
_____

Real Date: _____

STEP 2: SPEND WITHOUT WORRY ☀

Everyday journal what you purchased with a pretend $1,000. You can't save any money for the next day, you must use it in the day it is given. Everyday increase the amount by multiplying the amount from the day before by 2.

_____

_____

_____

_____

_____

_____

_____

_____

Total Purchased Today: $_____

Step 3: Receive ☀

"Everything that is in this journal, shall come to be."
Tell me if you see evidence of your pretend life in your real life. Be grateful and notice even the smallest evidence of the law of attraction. The more you are grateful and paying attention, the faster your desires will manifests.

"I have evidence of my abundance in my real life."

Real Date: _____

_____

_____

_____

_____

_____

_____

_____

_____

_____

_____

_____

STEP 1: PLAY PRETEND 🐝

Journal your entire day in great detail. Tell me how good your green juice was. Tell me what happened when you called your best friend.

_____
_____
_____
_____
_____
_____
_____
_____
_____
_____
_____
_____
_____
_____
_____
_____
_____
_____
_____
_____
_____
_____
_____
_____
_____
_____
_____
_____
_____
_____

Real Date: _____

STEP 2: SPEND WITHOUT WORRY ☀️

Everyday journal what you purchased with a pretend $1,000. You can't save any money for the next day, you must use it in the day it is given. Everyday increase the amount by multiplying the amount from the day before by 2.

_____
_____
_____
_____
_____
_____
_____
_____

_____

Total Purchased Today: $_____

Step 3: Receive 🌞

"Everything that is in this journal, shall come to be."

Tell me if you see evidence of your pretend life in your real life. Be grateful and notice even the smallest evidence of the law of attraction. The more you are grateful and paying attention, the faster your desires will manifests.

"I have evidence of my abundance in my real life."

Real Date: _____

_____
_____
_____
_____
_____
_____
_____
_____
_____
_____
_____
_____

STEP 1: PLAY PRETEND

Journal your entire day in great detail. Tell me how good your green juice was. Tell me what happened when you called your best friend.

_____

_____

_____

_____

_____

_____

_____

_____

_____

_____

_____

_____

_____

_____

_____

_____

_____

_____

_____

_____

_____

_____

_____

_____

_____

_____

_____

_____

_____

_____

_____

_____

Real Date: _____

STEP 2: SPEND WITHOUT WORRY ☀

Everyday journal what you purchased with a pretend $1,000. You can't save any money for the next day, you must use it in the day it is given. Everyday increase the amount by multiplying the amount from the day before by 2.

_____

_____

_____

_____

_____

_____

_____

_____

Total Purchased Today: $_____

Step 3: Receive ☀

"Everything that is in this journal, shall come to be."
Tell me if you see evidence of your pretend life in your real life. Be grateful and notice even the smallest evidence of the law of attraction. The more you are grateful and paying attention, the faster your desires will manifests.

"I have evidence of my abundance in my real life."

Real Date: _____

_____

_____

_____

_____

_____

_____

_____

_____

_____

_____

STEP 1: PLAY PRETEND

Journal your entire day in great detail. Tell me how good your green juice was. Tell me what happened when you called your best friend.

_____
_____
_____
_____
_____
_____
_____
_____
_____
_____
_____
_____
_____
_____
_____
_____
_____
_____
_____
_____
_____
_____
_____
_____
_____
_____
_____
_____

Real Date: _____

STEP 2: SPEND WITHOUT WORRY ☼

Everyday journal what you purchased with a pretend $1,000. You can't save any money for the next day, you must use it in the day it is given. Everyday increase the amount by multiplying the amount from the day before by 2.

_____

_____

_____

_____

_____

_____

_____

_____

Total Purchased Today: $_____

Step 3: Receive ☼

"Everything that is in this journal, shall come to be."

Tell me if you see evidence of your pretend life in your real life. Be grateful and notice even the smallest evidence of the law of attraction. The more you are grateful and paying attention, the faster your desires will manifests.

"I have evidence of my abundance in my real life."

Real Date: _____

_____

_____

_____

_____

_____

_____

_____

_____

_____

_____

_____

STEP 1: PLAY PRETEND 🐝

Journal your entire day in great detail. Tell me how good your green juice was. Tell me what happened when you called your best friend.

_____

_____

_____

_____

_____

_____

_____

_____

_____

_____

_____

_____

_____

_____

_____

_____

_____

_____

_____

_____

_____

_____

_____

_____

_____

_____

_____

_____

_____

Real Date: _____

STEP 2: SPEND WITHOUT WORRY ☀

Everyday journal what you purchased with a pretend $1,000. You can't save any money for the next day, you must use it in the day it is given. Everyday increase the amount by multiplying the amount from the day before by 2.

_____

_____

_____

_____

_____

_____

_____

_____

_____

Total Purchased Today: $_____

Step 3: Receive ☀

"Everything that is in this journal, shall come to be."
Tell me if you see evidence of your pretend life in your real life. Be grateful and notice even the smallest evidence of the law of attraction. The more you are grateful and paying attention, the faster your desires will manifests.

"I have evidence of my abundance in my real life."

Real Date: _____

_____

_____

_____

_____

_____

_____

_____

_____

_____

_____

_____

STEP 1: PLAY PRETEND 🐝

Journal your entire day in great detail. Tell me how good your green juice was. Tell me what happened when you called your best friend.

_____

_____

_____

_____

_____

_____

_____

_____

_____

_____

_____

_____

_____

_____

_____

_____

_____

_____

_____

_____

_____

_____

_____

_____

_____

_____

_____

_____

Real Date: _____

STEP 2: SPEND WITHOUT WORRY ☼

Everyday journal what you purchased with a pretend $1,000. You can't save any money for the next day, you must use it in the day it is given. Everyday increase the amount by multiplying the amount from the day before by 2.

_____
_____
_____
_____
_____
_____
_____
_____

Total Purchased Today: $_____

Step 3: Receive ☺

"Everything that is in this journal, shall come to be."
Tell me if you see evidence of your pretend life in your real life. Be grateful and notice even the smallest evidence of the law of attraction. The more you are grateful and paying attention, the faster your desires will manifests.

"I have evidence of my abundance in my real life."

Real Date: _____

_____
_____
_____
_____
_____
_____
_____
_____
_____
_____
_____

STEP 1: PLAY PRETEND

Journal your entire day in great detail. Tell me how good your green juice was. Tell me what happened when you called your best friend.

_____

_____

_____

_____

_____

_____

_____

_____

_____

_____

_____

_____

_____

_____

_____

_____

_____

_____

_____

_____

_____

_____

_____

_____

_____

_____

_____

_____

_____

_____

_____

_____

Real Date: _____

STEP 2: SPEND WITHOUT WORRY ☼

Everyday journal what you purchased with a pretend $1,000. You can't save any money for the next day, you must use it in the day it is given. Everyday increase the amount by multiplying the amount from the day before by 2.

_____

_____

_____

_____

_____

_____

_____

_____

Total Purchased Today: $_____

Step 3: Receive ☼

"Everything that is in this journal, shall come to be."
Tell me if you see evidence of your pretend life in your real life. Be grateful and notice even the smallest evidence of the law of attraction. The more you are grateful and paying attention, the faster your desires will manifests.

"I have evidence of my abundance in my real life."

Real Date: _____

_____

_____

_____

_____

_____

_____

_____

_____

_____

_____

STEP 1: PLAY PRETEND

Journal your entire day in great detail. Tell me how good your green juice was. Tell me what happened when you called your best friend.

_____
_____
_____
_____
_____
_____
_____
_____
_____
_____
_____
_____
_____
_____
_____
_____
_____
_____
_____
_____
_____
_____
_____
_____
_____
_____
_____
_____
_____
_____

Real Date: _____

STEP 2: SPEND WITHOUT WORRY ☀

Everyday journal what you purchased with a pretend $1,000. You can't save any money for the next day, you must use it in the day it is given. Everyday increase the amount by multiplying the amount from the day before by 2.

_____
_____
_____
_____
_____
_____
_____
_____

Total Purchased Today: $_____

Step 3: Receive ☀

"Everything that is in this journal, shall come to be."
Tell me if you see evidence of your pretend life in your real life. Be grateful and notice even the smallest evidence of the law of attraction. The more you are grateful and paying attention, the faster your desires will manifests.

"I have evidence of my abundance in my real life."

Real Date: _____

_____
_____
_____
_____
_____
_____
_____
_____
_____
_____
_____

STEP 1: PLAY PRETEND

Journal your entire day in great detail. Tell me how good your green juice was. Tell me what happened when you called your best friend.

_____

_____

_____

_____

_____

_____

_____

_____

_____

_____

_____

_____

_____

_____

_____

_____

_____

_____

_____

_____

_____

_____

_____

_____

_____

_____

_____

_____

_____

Real Date: _____

STEP 2: SPEND WITHOUT WORRY ☀

Everyday journal what you purchased with a pretend $1,000. You can't save any money for the next day, you must use it in the day it is given. Everyday increase the amount by multiplying the amount from the day before by 2.

_____

_____

_____

_____

_____

_____

_____

_____

_____

Total Purchased Today: $_____

Step 3: Receive ☀

"Everything that is in this journal, shall come to be."

Tell me if you see evidence of your pretend life in your real life. Be grateful and notice even the smallest evidence of the law of attraction. The more you are grateful and paying attention, the faster your desires will manifests.

"I have evidence of my abundance in my real life."

Real Date: _____

_____

_____

_____

_____

_____

_____

_____

_____

_____

_____

_____

STEP 1: PLAY PRETEND

Journal your entire day in great detail. Tell me how good your green juice was. Tell me what happened when you called your best friend.

_____
_____
_____
_____
_____
_____
_____
_____
_____
_____
_____
_____
_____
_____
_____
_____
_____
_____
_____
_____
_____
_____
_____
_____
_____
_____
_____
_____
_____
_____

Real Date: _____

STEP 2: SPEND WITHOUT WORRY ☀

Everyday journal what you purchased with a pretend $1,000. You can't save any money for the next day, you must use it in the day it is given. Everyday increase the amount by multiplying the amount from the day before by 2.

_____
_____
_____
_____
_____
_____
_____

_____

Total Purchased Today: $_____

Step 3: Receive ☀

"Everything that is in this journal, shall come to be."
Tell me if you see evidence of your pretend life in your real life. Be grateful and notice even the smallest evidence of the law of attraction. The more you are grateful and paying attention, the faster your desires will manifests.

"I have evidence of my abundance in my real life."

Real Date: _____

_____
_____
_____
_____
_____
_____
_____
_____
_____
_____
_____

STEP 1: PLAY PRETEND

Journal your entire day in great detail. Tell me how good your green juice was. Tell me what happened when you called your best friend.

_____
_____
_____
_____
_____
_____
_____
_____
_____
_____
_____
_____
_____
_____
_____
_____
_____
_____
_____
_____
_____
_____
_____
_____
_____
_____
_____
_____
_____
_____
_____
_____

Real Date: _____

STEP 2: SPEND WITHOUT WORRY ☀

Everyday journal what you purchased with a pretend $1,000. You can't save any money for the next day, you must use it in the day it is given. Everyday increase the amount by multiplying the amount from the day before by 2.

_____

_____

_____

_____

_____

_____

_____

_____

Total Purchased Today: $_____

Step 3: Receive ☀

"Everything that is in this journal, shall come to be."
Tell me if you see evidence of your pretend life in your real life. Be grateful and notice even the smallest evidence of the law of attraction. The more you are grateful and paying attention, the faster your desires will manifests.

"I have evidence of my abundance in my real life."

Real Date: _____

_____

_____

_____

_____

_____

_____

_____

_____

_____

_____

STEP 1: PLAY PRETEND 🐝

Journal your entire day in great detail. Tell me how good your green juice was. Tell me what happened when you called your best friend.

_____

_____

_____

_____

_____

_____

_____

_____

_____

_____

_____

_____

_____

_____

_____

_____

_____

_____

_____

_____

_____

_____

_____

_____

_____

_____

_____

_____

_____

_____

_____

Real Date: _____

STEP 2: SPEND WITHOUT WORRY ☼

Everyday journal what you purchased with a pretend $1,000. You can't save any money for the next day, you must use it in the day it is given. Everyday increase the amount by multiplying the amount from the day before by 2.

_____

_____

_____

_____

_____

_____

_____

_____

Total Purchased Today: $_____

Step 3: Receive ☺

"Everything that is in this journal, shall come to be."
Tell me if you see evidence of your pretend life in your real life. Be grateful and notice even the smallest evidence of the law of attraction. The more you are grateful and paying attention, the faster your desires will manifests.

"I have evidence of my abundance in my real life."

Real Date: _____

_____

_____

_____

_____

_____

_____

_____

_____

_____

_____

_____

STEP 1: PLAY PRETEND

Journal your entire day in great detail. Tell me how good your green juice was. Tell me what happened when you called your best friend.

_____
_____
_____
_____
_____
_____
_____
_____
_____
_____
_____
_____
_____
_____
_____
_____
_____
_____
_____
_____
_____
_____
_____
_____
_____
_____
_____
_____
_____
_____
_____

Real Date: _____

STEP 2: SPEND WITHOUT WORRY ☼

Everyday journal what you purchased with a pretend $1,000. You can't save any money for the next day, you must use it in the day it is given. Everyday increase the amount by multiplying the amount from the day before by 2.

_____

_____

_____

_____

_____

_____

_____

_____

Total Purchased Today: $_____

Step 3: Receive 🌐

"Everything that is in this journal, shall come to be."

Tell me if you see evidence of your pretend life in your real life. Be grateful and notice even the smallest evidence of the law of attraction. The more you are grateful and paying attention, the faster your desires will manifests.

"I have evidence of my abundance in my real life."

Real Date: _____

_____

_____

_____

_____

_____

_____

_____

_____

_____

_____

_____

STEP 1: PLAY PRETEND

Journal your entire day in great detail. Tell me how good your green juice was. Tell me what happened when you called your best friend.

_____
_____
_____
_____
_____
_____
_____
_____
_____
_____
_____
_____
_____
_____
_____
_____
_____
_____
_____
_____
_____
_____
_____
_____
_____
_____
_____
_____
_____
_____

Real Date: _____

STEP 2: SPEND WITHOUT WORRY ☼

Everyday journal what you purchased with a pretend $1,000. You can't save any money for the next day, you must use it in the day it is given. Everyday increase the amount by multiplying the amount from the day before by 2.

_____
_____
_____
_____
_____
_____
_____

_____

Total Purchased Today: $_____

Step 3: Receive ☺

"Everything that is in this journal, shall come to be."

Tell me if you see evidence of your pretend life in your real life. Be grateful and notice even the smallest evidence of the law of attraction. The more you are grateful and paying attention, the faster your desires will manifests.

"I have evidence of my abundance in my real life."

Real Date: _____

_____
_____
_____
_____
_____
_____
_____
_____
_____
_____
_____
_____

STEP 1: PLAY PRETEND

Journal your entire day in great detail. Tell me how good your green juice was. Tell me what happened when you called your best friend.

_____
_____
_____
_____
_____
_____
_____
_____
_____
_____
_____
_____
_____
_____
_____
_____
_____
_____
_____
_____
_____
_____
_____
_____
_____
_____
_____
_____
_____

Real Date: _____

STEP 2: SPEND WITHOUT WORRY ☼

Everyday journal what you purchased with a pretend $1,000. You can't save any money for the next day, you must use it in the day it is given. Everyday increase the amount by multiplying the amount from the day before by 2.

_____

_____

_____

_____

_____

_____

_____

_____

Total Purchased Today: $_____

Step 3: Receive ☼

"Everything that is in this journal, shall come to be."

Tell me if you see evidence of your pretend life in your real life. Be grateful and notice even the smallest evidence of the law of attraction. The more you are grateful and paying attention, the faster your desires will manifests.

"I have evidence of my abundance in my real life."

Real Date: _____

_____

_____

_____

_____

_____

_____

_____

_____

_____

_____

_____

STEP 1: PLAY PRETEND

Journal your entire day in great detail. Tell me how good your green juice was. Tell me what happened when you called your best friend.

_____

_____

_____

_____

_____

_____

_____

_____

_____

_____

_____

_____

_____

_____

_____

_____

_____

_____

_____

_____

_____

_____

_____

_____

_____

_____

_____

_____

_____

Real Date: _____

STEP 2: SPEND WITHOUT WORRY ☀

Everyday journal what you purchased with a pretend $1,000. You can't save any money for the next day, you must use it in the day it is given. Everyday increase the amount by multiplying the amount from the day before by 2.

_____

_____

_____

_____

_____

_____

_____

_____

Total Purchased Today: $_____

Step 3: Receive ☀

"Everything that is in this journal, shall come to be."
Tell me if you see evidence of your pretend life in your real life. Be grateful and notice even the smallest evidence of the law of attraction. The more you are grateful and paying attention, the faster your desires will manifests.

"I have evidence of my abundance in my real life."

Real Date: _____

_____

_____

_____

_____

_____

_____

_____

_____

_____

_____

_____

STEP 1: PLAY PRETEND

Journal your entire day in great detail. Tell me how good your green juice was. Tell me what happened when you called your best friend.

_____
_____
_____
_____
_____
_____
_____
_____
_____
_____
_____
_____
_____
_____
_____
_____
_____
_____
_____
_____
_____
_____
_____
_____
_____
_____
_____
_____
_____

Real Date: _____

STEP 2: SPEND WITHOUT WORRY ☼

Everyday journal what you purchased with a pretend $1,000. You can't save any money for the next day, you must use it in the day it is given. Everyday increase the amount by multiplying the amount from the day before by 2.

_____
_____
_____
_____
_____
_____
_____
_____

_____

Total Purchased Today: $_____

Step 3: Receive ☼

"Everything that is in this journal, shall come to be."
Tell me if you see evidence of your pretend life in your real life. Be grateful and notice even the smallest evidence of the law of attraction. The more you are grateful and paying attention, the faster your desires will manifests.

"I have evidence of my abundance in my real life."

Real Date: _____

_____
_____
_____
_____
_____
_____
_____
_____
_____
_____
_____

STEP 1: PLAY PRETEND 🐝

Journal your entire day in great detail. Tell me how good your green juice was. Tell me what happened when you called your best friend.

_____

_____

_____

_____

_____

_____

_____

_____

_____

_____

_____

_____

_____

_____

_____

_____

_____

_____

_____

_____

_____

_____

_____

_____

_____

_____

_____

_____

_____

_____

_____

_____

_____

Real Date: _____

STEP 2: SPEND WITHOUT WORRY ☀

Everyday journal what you purchased with a pretend $1,000. You can't save any money for the next day, you must use it in the day it is given. Everyday increase the amount by multiplying the amount from the day before by 2.

_____

_____

_____

_____

_____

_____

_____

_____

Total Purchased Today: $_____

Step 3: Receive ☀

"Everything that is in this journal, shall come to be."

Tell me if you see evidence of your pretend life in your real life. Be grateful and notice even the smallest evidence of the law of attraction. The more you are grateful and paying attention, the faster your desires will manifests.

"I have evidence of my abundance in my real life."

Real Date: _____

_____

_____

_____

_____

_____

_____

_____

_____

_____

_____

_____

STEP 1: PLAY PRETEND

Journal your entire day in great detail. Tell me how good your green juice was. Tell me what happened when you called your best friend.

_____

_____

_____

_____

_____

_____

_____

_____

_____

_____

_____

_____

_____

_____

_____

_____

_____

_____

_____

_____

_____

_____

_____

_____

_____

_____

_____

_____

_____

_____

Real Date: _____

STEP 2: SPEND WITHOUT WORRY ☼

Everyday journal what you purchased with a pretend $1,000. You can't save any money for the next day, you must use it in the day it is given. Everyday increase the amount by multiplying the amount from the day before by 2.

_____
_____
_____
_____
_____
_____
_____
_____

Total Purchased Today: $_____

Step 3: Receive ☼😊☼

"Everything that is in this journal, shall come to be."

Tell me if you see evidence of your pretend life in your real life. Be grateful and notice even the smallest evidence of the law of attraction. The more you are grateful and paying attention, the faster your desires will manifests.

"I have evidence of my abundance in my real life."

Real Date: _____

_____
_____
_____
_____
_____
_____
_____
_____
_____
_____
_____

STEP 1: PLAY PRETEND

Journal your entire day in great detail. Tell me how good your green juice was. Tell me what happened when you called your best friend.

_____
_____
_____
_____
_____
_____
_____
_____
_____
_____
_____
_____
_____
_____
_____
_____
_____
_____
_____
_____
_____
_____
_____
_____
_____
_____
_____
_____

Real Date: _____

STEP 2: SPEND WITHOUT WORRY ☼

Everyday journal what you purchased with a pretend $1,000. You can't save any money for the next day, you must use it in the day it is given. Everyday increase the amount by multiplying the amount from the day before by 2.

_____
_____
_____
_____
_____
_____
_____
_____

_____

Total Purchased Today: $_____

Step 3: Receive ☼

"Everything that is in this journal, shall come to be."

Tell me if you see evidence of your pretend life in your real life. Be grateful and notice even the smallest evidence of the law of attraction. The more you are grateful and paying attention, the faster your desires will manifests.

"I have evidence of my abundance in my real life."

Real Date: _____

_____
_____
_____
_____
_____
_____
_____
_____
_____
_____
_____

STEP 1: PLAY PRETEND

Journal your entire day in great detail. Tell me how good your green juice was. Tell me what happened when you called your best friend.

_____
_____
_____
_____
_____
_____
_____
_____
_____
_____
_____
_____
_____
_____
_____
_____
_____
_____
_____
_____
_____
_____
_____
_____
_____
_____
_____
_____

Real Date: _____

STEP 2: SPEND WITHOUT WORRY ☼

Everyday journal what you purchased with a pretend $1,000. You can't save any money for the next day, you must use it in the day it is given. Everyday increase the amount by multiplying the amount from the day before by 2.

_____

_____

_____

_____

_____

_____

_____

_____

Total Purchased Today: $_____

Step 3: Receive ☼

"Everything that is in this journal, shall come to be."
Tell me if you see evidence of your pretend life in your real life. Be grateful and notice even the smallest evidence of the law of attraction. The more you are grateful and paying attention, the faster your desires will manifests.

"I have evidence of my abundance in my real life."

Real Date: _____

_____

_____

_____

_____

_____

_____

_____

_____

_____

_____

_____

STEP 1: PLAY PRETEND 🐝

Journal your entire day in great detail. Tell me how good your green juice was. Tell me what happened when you called your best friend.

_____
_____
_____
_____
_____
_____
_____
_____
_____
_____
_____
_____
_____
_____
_____
_____
_____
_____
_____
_____
_____
_____
_____
_____
_____
_____
_____
_____
_____
_____
_____
_____

Real Date: _____

STEP 2: SPEND WITHOUT WORRY ☀

Everyday journal what you purchased with a pretend $1,000. You can't save any money for the next day, you must use it in the day it is given. Everyday increase the amount by multiplying the amount from the day before by 2.

_____
_____
_____
_____
_____
_____
_____
_____

Total Purchased Today: $_____

Step 3: Receive ☀

"Everything that is in this journal, shall come to be."

Tell me if you see evidence of your pretend life in your real life. Be grateful and notice even the smallest evidence of the law of attraction. The more you are grateful and paying attention, the faster your desires will manifests.

"I have evidence of my abundance in my real life."

Real Date: _____

_____
_____
_____
_____
_____
_____
_____
_____
_____
_____

STEP 1: PLAY PRETEND

Journal your entire day in great detail. Tell me how good your green juice was. Tell me what happened when you called your best friend.

_____

_____

_____

_____

_____

_____

_____

_____

_____

_____

_____

_____

_____

_____

_____

_____

_____

_____

_____

_____

_____

_____

_____

_____

_____

_____

_____

Real Date: _____

STEP 2: SPEND WITHOUT WORRY ☀

Everyday journal what you purchased with a pretend $1,000. You can't save any money for the next day, you must use it in the day it is given. Everyday increase the amount by multiplying the amount from the day before by 2.

_____
_____
_____
_____
_____
_____
_____
_____

Total Purchased Today: $_____

Step 3: Receive ☀

"Everything that is in this journal, shall come to be."

Tell me if you see evidence of your pretend life in your real life. Be grateful and notice even the smallest evidence of the law of attraction. The more you are grateful and paying attention, the faster your desires will manifests.

"I have evidence of my abundance in my real life."

Real Date: _____

_____
_____
_____
_____
_____
_____
_____
_____
_____
_____
_____

STEP 1: PLAY PRETEND

Journal your entire day in great detail. Tell me how good your green juice was. Tell me what happened when you called your best friend.

_____

_____

_____

_____

_____

_____

_____

_____

_____

_____

_____

_____

_____

_____

_____

_____

_____

_____

_____

_____

_____

_____

_____

_____

_____

_____

_____

_____

_____

_____

_____

Real Date: _____

STEP 2: SPEND WITHOUT WORRY ☼

Everyday journal what you purchased with a pretend $1,000. You can't save any money for the next day, you must use it in the day it is given. Everyday increase the amount by multiplying the amount from the day before by 2.

_____

_____

_____

_____

_____

_____

_____

_____

_____

Total Purchased Today: $_____

Step 3: Receive ☺

"Everything that is in this journal, shall come to be."
Tell me if you see evidence of your pretend life in your real life. Be grateful and notice even the smallest evidence of the law of attraction. The more you are grateful and paying attention, the faster your desires will manifests.

"I have evidence of my abundance in my real life."

Real Date: _____

_____

_____

_____

_____

_____

_____

_____

_____

_____

_____

_____

STEP 1: PLAY PRETEND

Journal your entire day in great detail. Tell me how good your green juice was. Tell me what happened when you called your best friend.

_____
_____
_____
_____
_____
_____
_____
_____
_____
_____
_____
_____
_____
_____
_____
_____
_____
_____
_____
_____
_____
_____
_____
_____
_____
_____
_____
_____
_____
_____
_____
_____

Real Date: _____

STEP 2: SPEND WITHOUT WORRY ☼

Everyday journal what you purchased with a pretend $1,000. You can't save any money for the next day, you must use it in the day it is given. Everyday increase the amount by multiplying the amount from the day before by 2.

_____
_____
_____
_____
_____
_____
_____
_____

_____

Total Purchased Today: $_____

Step 3: Receive ☼

"Everything that is in this journal, shall come to be."
Tell me if you see evidence of your pretend life in your real life. Be grateful and notice even the smallest evidence of the law of attraction. The more you are grateful and paying attention, the faster your desires will manifests.

"I have evidence of my abundance in my real life."

Real Date: _____

_____
_____
_____
_____
_____
_____
_____
_____
_____
_____
_____

STEP 1: PLAY PRETEND

Journal your entire day in great detail. Tell me how good your green juice was. Tell me what happened when you called your best friend.

_____

_____

_____

_____

_____

_____

_____

_____

_____

_____

_____

_____

_____

_____

_____

_____

_____

_____

_____

_____

_____

_____

_____

_____

_____

_____

_____

Real Date: _____

STEP 2: SPEND WITHOUT WORRY ☼

Everyday journal what you purchased with a pretend $1,000. You can't save any money for the next day, you must use it in the day it is given. Everyday increase the amount by multiplying the amount from the day before by 2.

_____
_____
_____
_____
_____
_____
_____
_____

Total Purchased Today: $_____

Step 3: Receive ☼

"Everything that is in this journal, shall come to be."
Tell me if you see evidence of your pretend life in your real life. Be grateful and notice even the smallest evidence of the law of attraction. The more you are grateful and paying attention, the faster your desires will manifests.

"I have evidence of my abundance in my real life."

Real Date: _____

_____
_____
_____
_____
_____
_____
_____
_____
_____
_____

STEP 1: PLAY PRETEND

Journal your entire day in great detail. Tell me how good your green juice was. Tell me what happened when you called your best friend.

_____

_____

_____

_____

_____

_____

_____

_____

_____

_____

_____

_____

_____

_____

_____

_____

_____

_____

_____

_____

_____

_____

_____

_____

_____

_____

_____

_____

Real Date: _____

STEP 2: SPEND WITHOUT WORRY ☀

Everyday journal what you purchased with a pretend $1,000. You can't save any money for the next day, you must use it in the day it is given. Everyday increase the amount by multiplying the amount from the day before by 2.

_____

_____

_____

_____

_____

_____

_____

_____

Total Purchased Today: $_____

Step 3: Receive ☀

"Everything that is in this journal, shall come to be."
Tell me if you see evidence of your pretend life in your real life. Be grateful and notice even the smallest evidence of the law of attraction. The more you are grateful and paying attention, the faster your desires will manifests.

"I have evidence of my abundance in my real life."

Real Date: _____

_____

_____

_____

_____

_____

_____

_____

_____

_____

_____

_____

STEP 1: PLAY PRETEND

Journal your entire day in great detail. Tell me how good your green juice was. Tell me what happened when you called your best friend.

_____

_____

_____

_____

_____

_____

_____

_____

_____

_____

_____

_____

_____

_____

_____

_____

_____

_____

_____

_____

_____

_____

_____

_____

_____

_____

_____

_____

_____

_____

Real Date: _____

STEP 2: SPEND WITHOUT WORRY ☼

Everyday journal what you purchased with a pretend $1,000. You can't save any money for the next day, you must use it in the day it is given. Everyday increase the amount by multiplying the amount from the day before by 2.

_____

_____

_____

_____

_____

_____

_____

_____

_____

Total Purchased Today: $_____

Step 3: Receive ☼

"Everything that is in this journal, shall come to be."
Tell me if you see evidence of your pretend life in your real life. Be grateful and notice even the smallest evidence of the law of attraction. The more you are grateful and paying attention, the faster your desires will manifests.

"I have evidence of my abundance in my real life."

Real Date: _____

_____

_____

_____

_____

_____

_____

_____

_____

_____

_____

_____

STEP 1: PLAY PRETEND

Journal your entire day in great detail. Tell me how good your green juice was. Tell me what happened when you called your best friend.

_____

_____

_____

_____

_____

_____

_____

_____

_____

_____

_____

_____

_____

_____

_____

_____

_____

_____

_____

_____

_____

_____

_____

_____

_____

_____

_____

_____

Real Date: _____

STEP 2: SPEND WITHOUT WORRY ☼

Everyday journal what you purchased with a pretend $1,000. You can't save any money for the next day, you must use it in the day it is given. Everyday increase the amount by multiplying the amount from the day before by 2.

_____
_____
_____
_____
_____
_____
_____
_____

Total Purchased Today: $_____

Step 3: Receive ☼

"Everything that is in this journal, shall come to be."
Tell me if you see evidence of your pretend life in your real life. Be grateful and notice even the smallest evidence of the law of attraction. The more you are grateful and paying attention, the faster your desires will manifests.

"I have evidence of my abundance in my real life."

Real Date: _____

_____
_____
_____
_____
_____
_____
_____
_____
_____
_____
_____

STEP 1: PLAY PRETEND

Journal your entire day in great detail. Tell me how good your green juice was. Tell me what happened when you called your best friend.

_____
_____
_____
_____
_____
_____
_____
_____
_____
_____
_____
_____
_____
_____
_____
_____
_____
_____
_____
_____
_____
_____
_____
_____
_____
_____
_____
_____

Real Date: _____

STEP 2: SPEND WITHOUT WORRY ☼

Everyday journal what you purchased with a pretend $1,000. You can't save any money for the next day, you must use it in the day it is given. Everyday increase the amount by multiplying the amount from the day before by 2.

_____

_____

_____

_____

_____

_____

_____

_____

Total Purchased Today: $_____

Step 3: Receive ☼

"Everything that is in this journal, shall come to be."
Tell me if you see evidence of your pretend life in your real life. Be grateful and notice even the smallest evidence of the law of attraction. The more you are grateful and paying attention, the faster your desires will manifests.

"I have evidence of my abundance in my real life."

Real Date: _____

_____

_____

_____

_____

_____

_____

_____

_____

_____

_____

_____

STEP 1: PLAY PRETEND

Journal your entire day in great detail. Tell me how good your green juice was. Tell me what happened when you called your best friend.

_____

_____

_____

_____

_____

_____

_____

_____

_____

_____

_____

_____

_____

_____

_____

_____

_____

_____

_____

_____

_____

_____

_____

_____

_____

_____

_____

_____

Real Date: _____

STEP 2: SPEND WITHOUT WORRY ☼

Everyday journal what you purchased with a pretend $1,000. You can't save any money for the next day, you must use it in the day it is given. Everyday increase the amount by multiplying the amount from the day before by 2.

_____

_____

_____

_____

_____

_____

_____

_____

_____

Total Purchased Today: $_____

Step 3: Receive ☼

"Everything that is in this journal, shall come to be."
Tell me if you see evidence of your pretend life in your real life. Be grateful and notice even the smallest evidence of the law of attraction. The more you are grateful and paying attention, the faster your desires will manifests.

"I have evidence of my abundance in my real life."

Real Date: _____

_____

_____

_____

_____

_____

_____

_____

_____

_____

_____

_____

STEP 1: PLAY PRETEND

Journal your entire day in great detail. Tell me how good your green juice was. Tell me what happened when you called your best friend.

_____
_____
_____
_____
_____
_____
_____
_____
_____
_____
_____
_____
_____
_____
_____
_____
_____
_____
_____
_____
_____
_____
_____
_____
_____
_____
_____
_____
_____
_____

Real Date: _____

STEP 2: SPEND WITHOUT WORRY ☼

Everyday journal what you purchased with a pretend $1,000. You can't save any money for the next day, you must use it in the day it is given. Everyday increase the amount by multiplying the amount from the day before by 2.

_____
_____
_____
_____
_____
_____
_____
_____

_____

Total Purchased Today: $_____

Step 3: Receive ☼

"Everything that is in this journal, shall come to be."

Tell me if you see evidence of your pretend life in your real life. Be grateful and notice even the smallest evidence of the law of attraction. The more you are grateful and paying attention, the faster your desires will manifests.

"I have evidence of my abundance in my real life."

Real Date: _____

_____
_____
_____
_____
_____
_____
_____
_____
_____
_____
_____
_____

STEP 1: PLAY PRETEND

Journal your entire day in great detail. Tell me how good your green juice was. Tell me what happened when you called your best friend.

_____

_____

_____

_____

_____

_____

_____

_____

_____

_____

_____

_____

_____

_____

_____

_____

_____

_____

_____

_____

_____

_____

_____

_____

_____

_____

_____

_____

_____

Real Date: _____

STEP 2: SPEND WITHOUT WORRY ☼

Everyday journal what you purchased with a pretend $1,000. You can't save any money for the next day, you must use it in the day it is given. Everyday increase the amount by multiplying the amount from the day before by 2.

_____
_____
_____
_____
_____
_____
_____
_____

_____

Total Purchased Today: $_____

Step 3: Receive ☼

"Everything that is in this journal, shall come to be."

Tell me if you see evidence of your pretend life in your real life. Be grateful and notice even the smallest evidence of the law of attraction. The more you are grateful and paying attention, the faster your desires will manifests.

"I have evidence of my abundance in my real life."

Real Date: _____

_____
_____
_____
_____
_____
_____
_____
_____
_____
_____
_____
_____

STEP 1: PLAY PRETEND

Journal your entire day in great detail. Tell me how good your green juice was. Tell me what happened when you called your best friend.

_____
_____
_____
_____
_____
_____
_____
_____
_____
_____
_____
_____
_____
_____
_____
_____
_____
_____
_____
_____
_____
_____
_____
_____
_____
_____
_____
_____
_____
_____
_____

Real Date: _____

STEP 2: SPEND WITHOUT WORRY ☀

Everyday journal what you purchased with a pretend $1,000. You can't save any money for the next day, you must use it in the day it is given. Everyday increase the amount by multiplying the amount from the day before by 2.

_____
_____
_____
_____
_____
_____
_____
_____

_____

Total Purchased Today: $_____

Step 3: Receive ☀

"Everything that is in this journal, shall come to be."

Tell me if you see evidence of your pretend life in your real life. Be grateful and notice even the smallest evidence of the law of attraction. The more you are grateful and paying attention, the faster your desires will manifests.

"I have evidence of my abundance in my real life."

Real Date: _____

_____
_____
_____
_____
_____
_____
_____
_____
_____
_____
_____

STEP 1: PLAY PRETEND

Journal your entire day in great detail. Tell me how good your green juice was. Tell me what happened when you called your best friend.

_____
_____
_____
_____
_____
_____
_____
_____
_____
_____
_____
_____
_____
_____
_____
_____
_____
_____
_____
_____
_____
_____
_____
_____
_____
_____
_____
_____
_____
_____

Real Date: _____

STEP 2: SPEND WITHOUT WORRY ☼

Everyday journal what you purchased with a pretend $1,000. You can't save any money for the next day, you must use it in the day it is given. Everyday increase the amount by multiplying the amount from the day before by 2.

_____
_____
_____
_____
_____
_____
_____
_____
_____

Total Purchased Today: $_____

Step 3: Receive ☼

"Everything that is in this journal, shall come to be."

Tell me if you see evidence of your pretend life in your real life. Be grateful and notice even the smallest evidence of the law of attraction. The more you are grateful and paying attention, the faster your desires will manifests.

"I have evidence of my abundance in my real life."

Real Date: _____

_____
_____
_____
_____
_____
_____
_____
_____
_____
_____
_____

Printed in Great Britain
by Amazon